Quotations from the Bible herein are taken variously from the King James Version of 1611 (KJV), the Revised Standard Version (RSV) copyright 1952 by the National Council of Churches of Christ, the Amplified Bible (Ampl) copyright 1964 and 1958 by Zondervan Publishing House and the Lockman Foundation, and the New American Standard Bible (NAS) copyright 1973 by the Lockman Foundation.

Dedication

To all of God's children who have been called Fatso, Tubby, or Two-by-Four, my fellow sufferers in life, especially those who have asked God to help them lose weight. I was an utter failure at weight loss until I found God's way, and He asked me to share it with you.

Contents

Acknowledgements

Special thanks to my husband Brooks, and our children Christa, Jolean, and Danny. They deserve a special crown of life for living with me before and after.

I praise God for our pastor, Merlin Carothers, and his wife, Mary. Merlin inspired and encouraged me to write this book. Mary inspires me to be more like her (and she loaned me her typewriter!).

Special appreciation goes to my friend and right arm, Pat Helps, who assists me in the ministry with talent and dedication, and to my friend, Irene Regis, seamstress and frequent babysitter for our family while I worked on the book. The love Jesus glows in them both.

Introduction

Would you believe I once had a charge account with a bakery truck? It was awful. I would buy a whole cake, carve off a piece and gobble it up. One thing led to another and before I knew it, half of the cake would be gone. I didn't want my family to know that I'd eaten half a cake all by myself, so under the circumstances there was only one thing to do. I ate the other half.

One whole cake down the tubes and out onto the hips. What did it get me? Self-hate and condemnation, that's what. By the time the family got home, I was touchy, irritable and in no mood to be pleasant. Not only was I hurting myself, I was hurting them as well.

And I wasn't alone. Over seventy-nine million people in the United States are overweight. I'm surprised somebody didn't start a "Food-Anon" long ago, not only for overweight people, but for their families too.

The bakery truck was only part of it. My whole life was centered on food. All I thought about was what to eat, when to eat, and, most of all, how much I could eat. I stuffed myself at mealtimes, and ate enormously all during the rest of the day. Even late at night, when the rest of the house was silent, you could still hear the slam of our refrigerator door. And the pounds kept piling on.

Needless to say, I wasn't happy with this state of affairs. I was very familiar with all sorts of diet books, but they never did me much good. I read them constantly, though, munching on goodies all the while, and then bored my friends half to distraction by my up-to-date reports on new diets, new doctors and new answers to the old problems of overweight and overeating. Later, I found that this sort of behavior is typical of fatties. I could talk a good diet, but I couldn't live it.

It got worse. When I heard of the by-pass operation, I thought that was the answer for me, and tried to arrange to have one. The doctor told me, however, that I wasn't fat enough! "Well, good," I thought. "I'll just gain another twenty pounds, have the operation, and then my problem will be solved." What a drastic remedy! I was willing to have my insides cut out in order to lose weight. I was ready to consent to major surgery rather than give up gorging myself day in and day out. That's how much a slave I was to food!

Meanwhile, I kept on eating. I also kept getting more miserable. After all, I was unhappy being fat, and hated the idea of getting fatter. But I couldn't get out of my predicament. I had tried almost every method there is to lose weight, and I had failed every time. After each try, I had put on more weight. It got so thoughts of food occupied all my waking hours.

Eating like this put me in a stupor. I couldn't see myself for what I was, and my mind was confused and divided against itself.

It took me a long time to find out, but I know now that's exactly where the battleground is—the mind. The battle of the bulge doesn't begin with the first drooling look at a piece of chocolate layer cake; or when the loaded fork is on its way to the mouth. It begins in the mind, and largely stays in the mind, not in the stomach. That's good news, because the mind can be healed by the good words of God, and it can gain mastery over the stomach.

If you have been overweight for very long, you know just

how hopeless this problem seems to be. If you are like me, you will have tried everything and you will be pretty discouraged with the results. You dieted, suffered, lost weight and gained it back again, usually with more besides. But there is good news for you: *the Holy Spirit helps our infirmities.* We can appropriate this power and apply it to our problem. We become Christians *believing* God, but we are made overcomers by *relying* on Him.

As you might have guessed by now, this is not just another book on dieting. The principles in this book have worked for me and they are working for a great number of others who are trying them. No, I'm not talking about dieting. I'm talking about overcoming, a way of life that, once learned, will stay with you.

Being fat is basically a sign that something is seriously wrong. It is a big cover-up and when we get serious about losing our cover, we will need a big exposure. We will need to admit that we need help, and we will have to expose our hidden faults to the healing power of God.

God's method is not a shortcut, but it is the shortest way to where we are going because it heals thoroughly, from the inside out. A slight healing is actually worse than no healing at all because it is deceptive. We think that we have something when actually we don't have nearly enough. The healing that really does the job will give us a new spirit (Christ's), and this spirit will retrain our flesh and give us a new mind (See Eph. 4:23 and Rom. 12:2).

When we became Christians, we came into an inheritance, and that inheritance included abundant life and self-control. If we have been living beneath our inheritance, that doesn't alter the fact that we have one. It's the same as if you didn't have the cash; it would merely mean that you needed a way to make a withdrawal. In this book, I want to relate as faithfully as I can the way God showed me how to make withdrawals from my spiritual bank account.

There is a song that includes the words". . . I want more of Jesus so I'll give Him more of me." That's really the secret. I thought I wanted to give Jesus more of me for years—but all I was giving away was what I basically didn't want—my fat. Sometimes I gave Him my word; but that wasn't very good. Every day ended like all the rest—in defeat and frustration—until I learned to withdraw the power in my heavenly bank account.

The uphill road we travel is especially discouraging and tiring to the overweight—unless you catch a ride in a powerful car. The word of God is that power. Finding what we need and using it to overcome our very real problem is what this book is about. God helped me to find the special vehicle that helped me to the top, and He told me to share it with you. So hop in! Welcome to an adventure in overcoming!

1 Honestly!

Telling it like it is . . . . it's no fun to be fat, and no glory to God.

Some books deal so successfully with success that they leave us in a state of despair. Victory doesn't come all at once. In fact, for me it took a long time just to get started.

When I was in church, the messages of victory and overcoming would minister to my heart, but once I got home, the idea of victory suddenly seemed a lot less attractive than the calorie-ridden treasures of our stuffed refrigerator. Food *now*, victory *later*, that was my motto. The problem was, I was never done eating. Victory was somewhere beyond the clouds, and the clouds were all made of whipped cream. Basically, the lusts of the flesh, the pleasures of the moment and the deceits of the heart had me in a snare. My *wanter* had not been changed. Sure, it could be inspired by the pastor's sermon, but when I

1

got home, alone, all it wanted was another piece of apple strudel.

My *wanter* also manifested itself more publicly.

When I first began the struggle, I taught a weight control class based on Scripture. Several were born again and showed real spiritual progress. Unfortunately, my weight also progressed; I gained ten pounds.

That was discouraging! How could I go on teaching weight control when I was getting fatter all the time? The inevitable happened. The ladies continued the Bible study and dropped the weight control part of it. I finally dropped the whole thing. To this day when someone mentions the weight control Bible study, I want to crawl under a chair and shiver.

A lot further along the road to success, I became embroiled in another major skirmish. The battleground in this case was a local hamburger stand that sold the best ice cream in town.

At the time, I was pleasantly aware that I had lost thirty pounds. People had complimented me on this accomplishment (I didn't mind that very much!) and, while I had every intention of holding on to my agreement with God, I must admit that my guard was down.

The battle began in a lovely restaurant on the harbor. My husband, Brooks, and I were celebrating our anniversary with a quiet dinner together. I wasn't gorging myself, either. I was enjoying the meal, and probably feeling a little smug about the fact that I was eating moderately with no intention of capping the dinner with a disastrous dessert.

Then it happened.

I suddenly noticed a waitress coming our way. She was holding a tray on which was perched the most fantastic hot fudge sundae I had ever seen. She couldn't be coming to our table! Or could she? Maybe Brooks had ordered this for me as a surprise. (I was good at making up such fantasies!)

Of course, this proved not to be the case. The waitress glided

2

right past our table and set the sundae down in front of another customer, who dug in instantly. Oh, murder! I asked Brooks if I could order one. He wisely replied that it was between the Lord and me. If I wanted one, he said, he would buy it for me.

Should I or shouldn't I? Could I or couldn't I? (After all, I had made this agreement with God.) What a struggle! Finally I made my decision. I would not give in to my flesh. No fudge sundae for me.

Victory! Hooray!

Not yet. It was only the end of round one. I couldn't get that sundae out of my mind. I kept thinking how good I had been, and how I deserved a reward. . . . We left for home, and I kept thinking of ice cream. By the time we reached the vicinity of the hamburger stand it was all over. We raced into the stand, made an emergency landing and ordered two sundaes.

There it was, in all its gooey glory. But I didn't feel very good about it at all. We were living in a small town, and by this time a number of people had heard my testimony and knew I was writing a book on weight loss. What if they were to see me now!

I felt like a drug dealer making a contact. We kept the car dark and I slouched down in my seat. What if somebody came past that I knew? Should I pretend I was somebody else? What if . . . ?

That wasn't all. As I ate the sundae, a nasty little voice began, "Isn't it good? You should have all you want, because you sure deserve it. You like it, don't you? You know, Joan, you should never have begun telling people that Jesus can set them free of gluttony. You shouldn't have to eat this delicious sundae all slouched down in the car, afraid that someone will see you! You're thinner now; go ahead and sit up. You've come a long way. . . ." (Sound familiar?)

Fortunately, I didn't pursue this line of thought very long. Instead, I began to think of the bondage of never ordering sundaes or gooey desserts again, because people would know who I was. What was I going to have to do, disguise myself in dark glasses and a big hat, and then lurk around ice cream shops two counties away? What a prospect!

Then the Lord said, "He who is free in the Son is free indeed" (John 8:36). I was free to do anything I wanted to do, really free! It didn't matter what other people said.

Suddenly I didn't want that sundae any more. I handed it to Brooks (who was surprised) and began thinking of what Jesus had done for me, because He wanted to. He was free; He didn't have to die on the cross. But He did.

I got so engrossed with thinking about what Jesus had done for me that I didn't notice what had happened. Victory had quietly begun to work for me. I was on the way to overcoming.

2 A Wrong Start

Look to the rock from which you were hewn. . . . Isaiah 51:1

Everybody wants to live an abundant life, but all a lot of us have is abundant fat. Too often we find that what we want to do, we don't do, and what we don't want to do, that we do. This is especially true of overeating; the harder we try to overcome, the more we eat. What's going on? We are willing to lose weight, but not willing to quit eating! I've never known a fat person who didn't want to lose weight, but I've known a ton (literally) who weren't willing to stop eating. We are looking for an easy way out, like a quick diet. What we really want is to hurry and lose weight so we can eat again; that's why quick diets never work. I've come to the conclusion that all fat people think this way. Like alcoholics, they know all the tricks!

The road to abundant life is not through tricks, but through truth. I want to begin by describing the winding road I had to travel before I found that truth, but let me emphasize that the retrospective part of our search should be a *short* one. You can learn from the past, *but don't live in it.*

The only time, until lately, that my weight was normal was when I was born, and that is when the problem started. My picture at age two tells the story. Fat little rich kid. Until I was eight, I lived in Altadena, California, the only foster child of a wealthy elderly couple. I was "it." Everything I wanted, I got. I was spoiled, I was fat, I was miserable. I remember my mother having me bend over in front of company to show off my cute little fat bottom. They all seemed to get a charge out of it. They felt the little rolls of fat covering my legs and exclaimed, "Isn't she cute?" So I thought I was cute, too, but that changed quickly enough when I was old enough to go to school. There I learned the truth. They laughed at my cute little fat self. I had had no contact with other children until school age, so it was quite a shock to encounter my peer group.

I could hardly wait to get home from my confrontation with this cruel world, but when I did it was only to learn that I would have to go back the next day, and the next, and face those terrible, mean kids again. School was here to stay.

Somewhere in childhood we begin to turn to food instead of people, and finally turn to food instead of our creator, God, with our problems. I think the day I started school and found out where I stood with the world was my day. Before that, I ate because my family thought it was cute for me to be fat, and plied me with goodies. Bless her heart, my foster mother was more then slightly plump, and kind and generous to a fault, but she failed to discipline me and plant within me the seed of wise living.

At school I discovered rejection. This was doubtless the day I began to set up my "altar," the cookie cupboard. An altar is a place to bring our problems and rejoice in our blessings. If we find ourselves at the cupboard or refrigerator when things go wrong we should ask, "Is this my altar?"

6

A Wrong Start

Soon after we begin to worship at this altar, we will find that we not only worship (eat) when we have problems, but when we are happy! Every day becomes some kind of celebration. It's amazing what the overeater can think of for a celebration. We have all kinds of special occasions, like the first day after Ground-hog Day. Or we feel put upon, and must reward ourselves by going out to eat.

In fairness to my foster mother, I should say that she was in her seventies at the time I am describing. Both my foster parents were brave and loving people, but they had been reared in a time when it was "healthy" to be fat, and they passed their eating habits on to me.

Many incidents reinforced this program of finding food as a solace. I remember one in particular. I was playing in our backyard with the little boy from across the street. He had dug a hole under the fence to come over and play with me. This was forbidden because my mother had heard him swear once, and placed a ban on his company. If she had only known what I said when she couldn't hear, she wouldn't have thought he was so bad! But mothers are usually somewhat blind and deaf. So the little boy and I saw each other fairly often in secret. He was seven and I was five. On this particular day we were sitting on a tree limb, out of sight. I noticed that his pants were unzipped. I had puzzled over the differences in the sexes and decided this was my chance to find out. I asked him what he had that I didn't. He obligingly showed me. This was very interesting, except for one thing: presto, like magic, there at the foot of the tree was my mother. God seems to always have mothers appear just when you wish they wouldn't.

In a most displeased voice I was told to get in the house before I got my neck broken and even more dire threats were directed at the little boy. We hastened to depart the scene. Once in the house I was overcome with guilt. It had all seemed quite innocent out there on the tree limb, but somehow dis-

7

covery made the situation look different. I had never seen my
mother so angry. After a while she called me into the kitchen,
and I went in fear and trembling, fully expecting to be offered
up to a neck breaking. But instead, she was feeling guilty about
the fierce way she had acted. Now she smoothed things over
with a piece of chocolate cake, complete with rich frosting and a
glass of cold milk. Chocolate cake was a favorite anyway, and as
an alternative to a broken neck, I definitely preferred it! I
learned something: why feel guilty and miserable when you
can reward yourself with cake and milk? I've resorted to this
reward many a time since then.

My bad eating habits were soon entrenched and my altar
firmly established. Food was my friend. It didn't appear to hurt
me (I learned better eventually), and people did hurt me. Right
here we have a beginning: recognize this pattern for what it is.
Food doesn't really get rid of the original hurt, but merely
buries it under a layer of fat, where the pain continues to gnaw
away, demanding more food. . . . There is no escape that
way!

When I was eight, my comfortable little world crumbled
about me. A beautiful young woman came to our door, and as it
was the maid's day out I answered. The pretty lady told me that
she was my real mother, and could she come in and visit? Now,
that was a shocker. Instead of one mother, I had two. I hadn't
known that my parents weren't my original set.

Soon I was living with my real parents. At first I was delighted to discover that I had three sisters besides another mom
and dad. Soon after I went to live with them, my dear foster
father died. My life was all mixed up and filled with hurt. I had
a hard time adjusting to my new old family. The three sisters
that had seemed so wonderful turned out to be "brats," or so I
thought. I had always had the whole cake, and now I had to
share it. I had had my own bedroom; now I had three room-

8

mates, and in summers I even had to share my twin bed with another. I had to share my toys; my foster parents had rented a small trailer to bring all my toys to my new home. And, worst of all, I had to share my new-found mother.

My parents had divorced when I was very young. My mother was unable to support four babies under the age of two-and-a-half, and even worse, had suffered a nervous collapse. My dad lived elsewhere and did not know what was going on. My great grandmother took my oldest sister, my grandmother took the twins, and my foster parents took me. They loved me and wanted to keep me, and my mother had agreed to it, thinking it best for me.

Seven years later my parents remarried each other and wanted their family back. They saw a judge who instructed them to take me immediately, because I had been with my foster family so long that to wait any longer would make a bad situation impossible. So they made what must have been a hard decision for them.

My life would have been very different if they had not included me in their re-formed family. But I feel now that they made the right decision, although I didn't then.

I was a spoiled, selfish eight-year-old. It's hard enough to love an eight-year-old, but one who is a stranger and has never been disciplined, forget it! But they didn't forget it. They lived out what was a very hard year for all of us.

Now I love both sets of parents and think it a blessing to have more parents than the average, but I didn't think it then, and I must confess that I did my best at that time to make my parents pay for what they'd done to me. I was miserable and I wanted everyone else to be miserable with me. And believe me, they were.

My own mother had a weight problem, too. I came from a line of chubbies on both sides. My grandfather Ahrens weighed over 350 pounds when he died. It was probably closer to 400, but after a while you can't weigh, and who wants to anyway when you have to go to the baggage scale to do your deed? Dad's mother was over 225 pounds, and the list goes on.

3 Program for Disaster

My childhood, where the computer gets programmed to perpetuate itself:

My childhood and youth were plagued with the familiar taunt, "Fatty, fatty, two-by-four, can't get through the kitchen door." Now, that just wasn't true. If there was any door I *could* get through, it was the kitchen door.

It seems to me I was always the fattest kid in the class, the fattest kid in the neighborhood, the fattest kid in the family, and the fattest kid on the bus. Another girl on the bus came in a close second, and it may have been a tie. Her name was Geneva, and we were good friends. We shared everything except our food; hers was hers and mine was mine. Every year we rode the same bus and shared a seat, a tight squeeze.

The last day of school always found us having the same

conversation as the year before. It went like this, "Next year when I come back I'm going to be so thin no one will recognize me." She would answer, "I'm going on a diet *tomorrow.*" Note that diets always start tomorrow! "Me, too," I answered. But the first day of school would find us even more tightly squeezed into the same seat. Oh, we had been on lots of diets, one nearly every day. While we laughed at ourselves on the outside, we cried on the inside. Another year of "fatty, fatty, two-by-four. . . ."

When the kids decided to have a neighborhood circus, guess who was the fat lady? How demoralizing, how awful; but it's true. What else could I be? My oldest sister, Terry, was in charge of the circus, so I couldn't get out of it. I tried, but I ended up sitting there on the bench with the kids walking by and poking me and saying, "Is that all you? Do you have a pillow in there? You couldn't be that fat!" Ha, ha. Sure, I had a pillow in front, but the one in back was all me. Right after this terrible experience, I spent all the money I made at the circus on something to eat.

My problem was that I was a people-pleaser. I wanted everyone to like me. I *had* to be funny and laugh when they made fun of me. But I didn't have to share my candy with them, so I ate it all after a hard day's work of being laughed at and expected to laugh back.

By third grade, my parents had become concerned. They took me to a diet doctor who gave me tests. My favorite doctor was the one across from the Lido Drug Store, because every week after my visit I'd have a double-dip cone. After all, I deserved it, so I thought. This guy tried to scare the weight off me. Needless to say, that didn't work for long. Again in seventh grade I made the pilgrimage to a weight doctor. I weighed in at the grand total of 177 pounds. He told me I would die if I didn't lose weight soon, and even mentioned that he thought my bones would soon be crushed under the weight! I thought that would be neat. I tried to picture a leg that was nicely skinny because the bone was crushed. The idea of dying did scare me for a while, and I remember announcing this to my friends as I was eating cake. I concluded that if I had to die, and I would sooner or later, I would rather eat myself to death than go any other way. I did want to lose weight, but I didn't want to quit eating.

I remember once when I went to bed early—that in itself made my dad suspicious—because I had bought goodies with babysitting money. I snuggled into bed and opened my package of cookies. Dad passed by and heard the rustle of cellophane. He opened the door and asked what I was doing. I almost strangled swallowing a whole cookie. Now, a cookie or two my dad could understand, but a whole package was too much! He was livid. He ordered me to the kitchen. He was going to make me eat the whole package. That was fine with me, as that was what I was going to do anyway. I obediently ate away, trying not to show how delighted I was, Suddenly he yelled, "Stop. For crying out loud, I can see this won't work." He didn't know how to handle me, and I can't blame him, for I didn't know how to handle myself. Food wasn't just my altar; it was my life. I was in bondage.

My mom sometimes asked me the question I would later ask my own kids: "Joan, am I as fat as Mrs. . . . ?" What can you say to your own mother? It's not wise to let the whole truth be known; after all, she cooks your meals! And if *she* were to go on a diet. . . . So I always said, "No, mom, she's lots fatter than you are!"

That's what mothers like to hear. If we really want the truth, we shouldn't ask someone who will flatter us, we should ask an unbiased party, like a doctor. He gets paid for being honest. Of course, when the truth is told, we don't like it. Dumb doctor,

13

what does he know? How can he possibly understand . . . he's skinny as a rail. Or, if he isn't, we say, "Huh, where does he get off telling *me* to go on a diet?"

Unfortunately, even when we listen to the doctor and try to diet, we still have very little success. Don't blame the doctor; he's using all his talent, and he'll be the first to admit that the medical profession doesn't have all the answers on permanent and successful weight control. Most doctors are equipped to deal with physical and, sometimes, emotional problems, but seldom with the spiritual. Dr. Dorian Paskowitz has stated that 100% of people who diet seriously lose weight, but only 2% keep it off over a one-year period.

The doctor who made me maddest actually helped me most. Our family physician was a fine doctor and an excellent surgeon, but what was he to do with this thirty-one-year-old woman who was crying in his office because she was so fat? I wanted another diet, or better yet, a shot or pill, anything. He was extremely thin, and I think I made him a little ill. He said, "Joan, you are a very spiritual person. Why can't you take that power and apply it to this area of your life?"

The truth always hurts, and I could feel my face turn red as tears of hurt and anger ran down my cheeks to wash away the tears of self-pity. What I should have said is, "Thank you, doctor! That's just what I needed." Instead I sat there seething to myself, "You big dummy. If I knew how to do that, I wouldn't be here asking *you* what to do."

I left the office feeling worse than ever. I'd come to him for an answer and left with another question. But the question began to bug me. "Why can't I apply God's power to overcome my eating problems? I ask God for power in every other area of life, and He is always faithful. Why not this one?" So that doctor unlocked the secret, after all. He pointed me to God, and I asked Him, and He pointed the way, as you will see.

14

4 The Days of My Youth

Teenage years . . . often miserable at best, and impossible at worst, which includes fat kids.

Yuk! That's for my teenage years. I always worked after school and on weekends. And, somehow, I always found a job around food. I wonder how that happened? Office work just didn't attract me.

During my sophomore year, I starved down to 145 pounds. This was as close to a miracle as I had ever come. I had just lost my tonsils and couldn't swallow, which probably accounts for it. I felt thin and very proud. Then I got a job at the local theater as the "candy girl." The pay was low, but I could eat lots. The theater lost money on that deal! I gained thirty pounds in a few months, leaving a trail of candy wrappers that nearly clogged the aisles.

The stockroom was best, for my eating wasn't disturbed by customers. David said "Thou knowest my foolishness and my sins are not hid from thee" (Psalm 69:5). How true! We may think that what we eat in private doesn't count, but it begins to show in public.

The world swam by—danced by—ran by, and I just sat there, getting fatter. Did you sit there with me? Are you still sitting there?

Talk about a wallflower! Everything I wanted to do, I couldn't do, because I was too fat. I decided to brave it once, and took up swimming. I laughed at myself and got in the water as fast as I could, and stayed until dark. This gave me a good appetite, so I always ate extra after a swim. My fat body was the boss. It ran my life, and I hated it.

John Wesley asked his mother for a definition of sin, and her reply was: "Whatever increases desire for more of itself and less of Christ, to you that is sin." Words of wisdom! For all my teenage years my body dictated where I would go, when I would go, and even with whom. Only those who would be seen with me, that's who! Boys were afraid of me. If anyone gave me a hard time, I just hit them. My dad used to say there wasn't a man alive good enough to touch me, and I added, there wasn't one big enough either. I didn't laugh.

My actions didn't show it at that time, but I had asked Christ into my heart at a church service when I was twelve. The people in that church were happy, and I wanted what they had. They accepted me and loved me as I was, but my dad had seen old-time "holy roller" meetings and vowed that his daughter was not going to be seen at such a church, and he forbade me to go. So I sneaked to church, which didn't sit well with him. But I knew nothing then about obedience or submission. My dad didn't listen to me when I told him about the Lord, but if I had mopped the kitchen floor without being asked, he might have heard it loud and clear. What a rebellious mess I was!

I was practically a juvenile delinquent in junior high school. My parents sent me away to my great grandmother, who was supposed to straighten me out. I returned two weeks later a different girl, and to be honest I must say that Nanny (our pet name for her) was never the same either. For one thing, I detested vegetables, especially peas and, Lord forbid, eggplant. That was doubly gross! So Nanny decided that eggplant would be a good place to start. We entered into a royal battle and she won. She won some ground at the table, all right, but Nanny was so old she couldn't go downstairs to the basement where she kept all her home-canned goodies. I devoured one jar of mincemeat, a quart jar as I remember, among other things, and needless to say I returned home plumper than ever, and Nanny couldn't figure it out, until a few months later when she made it to the basement.

I was glad to get home. And I was still letting life pass me by when I graduated from high school at age sixteen. During those years I followed the yo-yo syndrome, losing a little weight and then gaining more. My boyfriends would come and go. They came when I lost and left when I gained. I had a few steadies who thought that I had such a winning personality that they could overlook my plumpness. But if one of them had asked me to choose between him and a thick malt, the malt would have won.

Then there came a day when I heard a car zoom by my house. I got a good look at the boy driving that car. Wow. He was it! He didn't see me, not 'fer nuthin'. So I began to diet, a fast crash diet. I spent many hours watering the lawn, hoping he would drive by. Our yard improved immensely that summer. I looked better, too, I must admit.

Then it happened. He came to my house and asked me to go

17

for a coke with him. I was in love; I must have been—I didn't drink the coke!

The first time he kissed me, I knew that this was the boy I must marry. He accepted me as I was. We didn't go to the beach together, because he knew I felt uncomfortable there. He was so kind, just the man I had been saving myself for (and there was a lot of me to save). I chased him until he caught me. He liked my eyes and my face. He saw past my chubby body.

He was definitely a face man, and that was good. People had always said I had a pretty face. In fact, so many people said, "You have such a pretty face; if you'd only lose weight, you'd be pretty," I wanted to stuff a banana up their nose and say "You'd be pretty too if you'd just take that banana out of your face." It's as if people are afraid that you'll live all your life and not know you're fat!

5 We Two Are One

Marriage . . . I didn't think it would happen!

So the handsome young man loved a "pretty face" and we got married. His name was Brooks Cavanaugh. The old saying that love is blind certainly proved true for us. I was seventeen and he was nineteen. He was well on his way to alcoholism. He was drinking at work and taking pills. I was at home eating my troubles away (or eating them on), and I began to think about God. I knew there had to be more to life than we were experiencing so far: fighting, spending money, drinking and gorging on food.

My first pregnancy terminated with a stillborn baby, a girl who would have been blind and deaf. I had worked in a state hospital for the retarded, and this all combined to give me nightmares; I dreamed of rooms full of retarded, deformed children and they were all mine. I would wake up screaming. I couldn't cope with it.

I was soon pregnant again and before Christa was born in June, 1961, I began to pray. One day when Oral Roberts was on TV, he said if you wanted a healing for yourself or someone else, to put your hands on the TV and pray with him. By this time I was crying like a baby, and I did as he said. I asked God to forgive all my sins and to make my unborn baby healthy. The healing that I really needed was for myself. I had rebelled against God in every way. But He was patient and brought me unto Himself, even though I dragged my heels most of the way.

When Christa was nine months old I came into a new relationship with Christ. I waddled down the aisle of a little church and asked to be baptized in water that very day. Those dear people were more than glad to oblige and the baptismal font was ready and waiting. All they had to do was find someone big enough to hold my 230 pound frame up. There was only one man big enough to do the job and by the time we both had gotten in and out of that water, most of it had oozed up and over the side into the overflow.

This was the best day of my life. It was a new beginning. "Now is the good time; Now is the day" (2 Cor. 6:2). My new life in Christ began growing, but I'm sorry to say that my body kept growing, too. I was happy with my new experience, but disgusted with myself. All this time I had been going to diet doctors, reducing salons, and trying weird diets. I would lose weight, but gain it back along with more. I detested the word "obese." That is what doctors call you if you are more than a few pounds overweight. Somehow I had never thought of myself as an obese person until one day a doctor wounded me with that awful word. It sounds like "obscene." The doctor was speaking into a tape recorder, giving my name, age, and these awful words, "obese female Caucasian weighing 230 pounds." Impossible as it seems, I had never thought of myself as "obese."

It is demoralizing to be stripped naked when you are over-weight anyway, let alone called a dirty five-letter word. I clutched my hospital gown, which was no better than a sanforized hanky, and I wanted to die.

Some people believe that overeating is carrying out the death wish, and it may be true. It's for sure that part of me died that day in the doctor's office. But he did accomplish this much: he made me take a good look at myself.

One of the ways we fatties "ease our path" is with lots of laughter. Only *we* know how we really feel! When I weighed 230 pounds I found it easier to make fun of myself first before someone else got the chance. I remember telling my friends that I'd get a whiplash every time I removed my girdle. They laughed, but I nearly cried every time I put it on. I detested those longline garments. I squeezed myself into those awful things to hide some of my fat from the world, regardless of the permanent scars they left in my side.

You may remember the TV commercial about the 18-hour girdle. I always got a laugh when I told friends that my 18-hour girdle self-destructed in five hours. But what really self-destructed was my self-esteem. My body was the temple of the Holy Spirit, and if I had been Him, I would have moved out. But God's gift is not that way. His love is steady.

I couldn't hide from myself, nor could I hide from God. He wasn't really impressed with my girdle one way or another. What He wanted was my obedience, and that was more than I knew how to give.

6 Whoops—Back to Two

Marriage On The Rocks . . . the program for disaster takes its toll.

After Christa's birth, I had a miscarriage, and then another little daughter came. This baby seemed like an angel from heaven. She didn't have wings, but she did seem to have a slight halo. Her name was Jolean Lee, and Brooks and I loved her to distraction. Christa ignored her and managed quite well for about two weeks. Then one day while I was hanging out clothes, Christa decided to welcome Jolean into the family by picking her up by the neck. It's hard to move fast when you weigh 230, but I outdid myself that day.

The toxemia that I'd had during pregnancy stayed with me. I kept saying to myself, "What are you doing to your body, Joan?" The answer came, "Killing it, that's what." During this time, which seemed like one long pregnancy, I gained and lost and gained again, always ending with a gain. I had the most fantastic doctor in the world. He didn't yell at me when I gained weight. I liked him, needless to say. Furthermore, he never prescribed a diet for any of his patients without putting himself on it first. He put me on a fast after the baby came, permitting only fruit juice and skimmed milk. I knew that he'd done it himself, and I didn't want to remain in this toxic state, so I yielded.

This time I actually stayed on the diet. It lasted two weeks and was a real beginning. I found I was not going to expire during the night even when I didn't stuff my jaws before going to bed. My dad used to ask me, when I was stuffing at bedtime, if I thought I would starve to death before morning. I didn't think it was funny at the time. I do think that I was so poor and wretched, spiritually speaking, that I was afraid that someone else would eat the food before I could get mine (and usually theirs too). It was my heart that was hungry, but all I could think to do was feed my face. The food entered my body and was perverted into fat to show the world that I ate too much.

In spite of our two darling girls, our marriage of five years was still miserable. Christ had done much for us separately. My husband had quit drinking and smoking, and so had I, but we were still too immature to realize that marriage is not a partner-ship, but a "oneship," each 100% for the other, even if the other is not 100% for you at the time. Marriage is to quit being two and start becoming one. It's like a heart transplant; it hurts. Infections rise up. The patient has to be watched. Neither of us were "patient," real or otherwise.

I must admit that if our input at this time were to be meas-ured, Brooks would win. He deserves a crown for putting up with me and continuing to love me when I was most unlovable. I didn't like myself and wasn't exactly brimming with affection and warmth toward Brooks.

We were hypocrites, actors (that's what hypocrite means).

We pretended to be happy, but we weren't. We fought constantly, except at church, of course. We didn't want people to get the wrong idea, which would have been the right idea. Of course, every time we fought, I had an excuse to be upset, and naturally I had to eat when I was upset. (I also ate when I wasn't upset.) I wouldn't be surprised if I started most of those fights so I could blame all my problems on Brooks and have an excuse to eat.

Some of us seem to take longer to learn than others, and I was one of those. Since I was crippled by self-hate, it isn't any wonder that our love did not grow, but began to shrivel. Both Brooks and I realized that it would take a miracle to heal our self-inflicted unhappiness. But we still needed to learn that we had chosen to be unhappy, and that we must choose otherwise.

But this experience was still ahead of us. Self-hate is a whole field full of stones to stumble over. I was a prisoner of my fat and took my self-hate out on my spouse. I began to accuse Brooks of loving another girl. I know that he did, for he told me that he loved the girl I used to be when we first married. But that girl had gone to prison—in her own body.

Late one night—it was actually two o'clock in the morning—we were fighting. Most people sleep at that hour, but fighting is a cancer that spreads like wildfire and knows no discipline. I accused Brooks of not loving me any more. His standard reply had been "Yes I do, honey"—what else do you tell a wife who outweighs you by sixty-five pounds? But that night he put his cards on the table, "You're right, Joan, I don't love you any more."

What I had really been asking Brooks all those years was, "I don't find anything lovable in me; can you see something in me worth loving?" When he finally answered "No," I was crushed, broken, completely destroyed. I was so undone I didn't even eat! That's really something. Probably the first time it ever happened.

For once, instead of turning to my self-made altar, the refrigerator, I turned to God. I cried my heart out and confessed to Him that I'd come to the end of myself. I told Him I really did love my husband and didn't want to lose him. How could I stop myself from losing everything, including my sanity?

God let me see how completely I had torn asunder the love with which we had begun our marriage. But He said not to worry; that He would give us new love for each other, a real love that would be far better than we had before. This would be *His love*, and it would grow from a small seed into a beautiful tree that others could sit under and enjoy its shade. God knows when we finally mean business, and then He speaks.

7 A Pilgrim's Nonprogress

A walk down Folly Avenue, where you find all the things that don't work.

Most programs to lose weight don't work permanently for most people. A short look at them will help us realize why not.

During my childhood I dreamed I would wake up some morning thin and beautiful, and no one would recognize me. To be honest, I also dreamed this when I grew up. I wanted an easy way out, one with no pain or self-denial. It sounded good but never came true, I didn't wake up thin, instead I grew fat. Deut. 31:15 says "You became fat, you grew thick. . . ." Note that it says you *grew* fat; I didn't wake up one morning suddenly fat, but for some reason that's how fat people want their problem to disappear—overnight. Thus they are subject

to every fad or magic potion offered, and a horde of entre-
preneurs get rich from our magic dream. That is about all that
happens: they get rich, we stay fat.

Most of the people who read this book will probably have
tried many diets and gimmicks. But just in case you are new to
the old diet trail, let me tell you what the world offers in this
line. The first time I lost weight was in a diet club. I used pills,
shots, water pills, and laxatives. I starved all week, took a water
pill and a laxative, then after a busy day in the bathroom,
weighed in at the meeting. Afterward we "girls" in the club
went out and stuffed ourselves with all the things we had been
denied for six days. We needed a little reward for having been
so good all week! (Our hearts deceive us so we can't see
ourselves as others do.)

During these days I tried all the fad diets I came across.
Through sheer determination and a lot of foolish procedures
that damaged my body, I lost eighty pounds. I was literally
chiseled out, and believe me, it hurt. And my triumph was
short-lived. Like all the projects we undertake using the wrong
methods with the wrong motives, it failed. The trouble with
putting up the fight in my strength alone, without the use of
God's power tools, was that I was depending on a mighty
undependable person—myself.

At this time I got pregnant again. We had wanted another
baby, and we were thinking of an adoption. As it turned out, I
gave birth to our only son, Danny Brooks, and we are delighted
we have him. But the news of another pregnancy threw me into
despair. It is not only easy to gain weight when you're pregnant, it is difficult not to, and I was soon fat again. With my
typical glutton's reasoning, I let myself eat, figuring I would
have to diet anyway after the baby was born. That's about as
reasonable as an alcoholic getting drunk because he will have to
sober up tomorrow. Overeaters don't think clearly,* partly

---

* Sugar is absorbed immediately by body tissues, having an effect similar to that of alcohol.

because the high-sugar, high-carbohydrate foods they love have a stupefying effect on their brains.

The first Sunday I went to church after Danny was born, some thoughtless soul looked at my fat body stuffed into a tight suit and remarked, "I thought you already had the baby." Danny turned out to be the best baby in the world, but my poor body was as fat as it had ever been. Danny weighed seven pounds at birth and I weighed 190! What a feeling! If you were a carpenter and had built a beautiful house, only to find it some morning torn to the ground, how would you feel? I felt awful.

I grasped at straws and went to doctor after doctor. A doctor who specialized in internal medicine saw a bit beyond my body. He said he didn't think I was emotionally ready to be thin. "Your fat is covering up more than your bones." He was right. I wasn't ready to be thin, but I wasn't ready to be fat either, which, like it or not, I was.

The next six years I continued the yo-yo syndrome. Many times I dieted, but always ended with my weight more than when I started. My spirits were lower than the scale could go. What a life, up and down and in and out, much like an accordion—according to what I ate.

People who have tried it agree that fasting is easier than eating with control. I could fast, but when I started eating again, look out! With fasting, there's only one decision to make: eat or don't eat. Eating with control involves many decisions during the day, and at night too. Fasting works for other things; once I fasted for three days and God did something special in the life of every person I prayed for. As a state of humility, it is a fine way to pursue Christian virtues, but as a way to lose weight, I don't recommend it. There are times when you should *not* fast; if you do it, read a good book on the subject and know what you're doing. My eating was compulsive; I was in bondage to food, so fasting only aggravated my condition.

A lot of our eating is for comfort or the strength to "face life." When an alcoholic goes into a bar for a drink so he can face life, you know what happens. To say nothing of the time he loses, he manages in the drunken state to add embarrassments and guilt to his burden, and sometimes broken laws that have to be faced and paid for in a cold courtroom. Now he is more impoverished than ever, and life is even more complex! It's the same for the glutton. If overweight is bugging you, more of it won't cure you. We know that, of course, but we choose to forget it while the urge to eat is upon us. Eating may "cover" distress, but any "comfort" derived is temporary and self-defeating.

Just as we eat for the wrong reasons, we tend to diet for the wrong reasons. One woman told me she wanted to lose weight so she could go into a candy shop and buy and eat without having people stare disapprovingly. No! That's the wrong reason to lose weight. We need to find our comfort in better places than candy stores, to put our trust in something higher than the "beggarly elements" that wrought the damage in the first place.

Gently, the Lord was getting through to me. I read "In freedom did Christ set us free; stand fast therefore and be not entangled again in a yoke of bondage" (Gal. 5:1). Now I was getting somewhere. I asked Jesus for more of Himself, more of His love, more of His Spirit, more of His power to overcome. He began putting my life together again, including my over-burdened body. It was not easy; overcoming is not easy until you get the hang of it, but it is the only permanent answer. A life of victory is God's will for us.

If only I could say that from then on I simply fell into victory, but that was not the case. I kept getting in the way. As I said, I'm a slow learner! God's ways may be a mystery to us, but ours are an open book to Him! I would pray for deliverance from the fat I hated, then go straight to the kitchen for sweets and snacks. My spirit was willing, but my flesh was weak; in fact, it was just plain out of control. I would prefer to leave out the next part of my story, but I want you to know that no matter where you're at, there is hope!

In 1973 I went to yet another weight-control group, and since it had it's beginning in biblical principles I thought surely it was the answer. They used Scripture and a lot of things God had already shown me, but I didn't have it all together even yet. I would go without sugars and flours like the group said, then suddenly let go and gorge myself. It was awful. One bite of a no-no was all it took. Even thinking about it was enough to start the action of overeating. In a way I was worse off than ever; now when I started to eat, there seemed to be no stopping.

"The heart is deceitful above all things and desperately wicked, who can know it?" (Jer. 17:9). Let me illustrate. At this time, a dazzling *religious* idea occurred to me, and I thought I really had the answer: manipulating God. Our pastor has a special ministry on praising the Lord for problems. Brooks and I had read about and practiced praise, with many wonderful results. One day as our pastor spoke on this subject, the idea occurred to me that there was one thing I had never praised God for—my fat. I hated it so, and hated myself for having it. Well, here was a way out! I would praise God for my fat, and that would make me lose weight.

As soon as I got home, I started praising God for being fat, then I polished off the dessert plate. I had a great time, for a while, praising up a storm. I could picture myself eating all I wanted and what I wanted while wearing a size ten. I even ate a banana split in public; if anyone sneered at me, I was going to quote Scripture: "There is therefore now no condemnation to them that are in Christ Jesus." I told Brooks, in between bites,

31

that I was through worrying about fat. He looked puzzled, but tried to be happy that perhaps this burden of my life was being lifted.

Only one thing was wrong with this: it didn't work. A third chin began to undergird my double chin. Brooks looked more than puzzled; he looked worried. But I was a stubborn case. I was sure God wouldn't let me down. I had missed hearing the law that says, "whatsoever a man sows, that also shall he reap." This law includes ice cream and candy! Not only do you reap, you begin to rip. When my new slacks that had fit so well began to split, I planted my two feet on the scale. I had to pry my eyes open. Twenty pounds gained in one month!

Disgust follows when a person sees how his own heart has deceived him into going his own foolish way. If I hadn't been so engrossed in my own way of operating, I surely would have seen how wrongheaded my thinking was. I did have sense enough to realize that the fault had to be mine, not that of our good pastor, and surely not God's. So I came back to my friend, Jesus, and I prayed, "Lord, forgive me. Open my ears that I may hear your truth, and open my eyes that I might see my sin as you see it." He answers prayers of distress. He forgave me, He opened my ears, and when I began to hear, He led me onward.

Have you ever noticed how God presses a lesson home when we are ready to hear? This is what I heard: "We have victory *in Christ Jesus*. The battle is won; your part is to enlist and get under the authority of the right Commander, *then* you can claim the rewards of the victor." Every tape I listened to said it, every book I read mentioned it, every sermon touched on it, and finally I said, "Yes, Lord, I get the message." I struggled some, oh yes, the flesh is obstinate! I can understand why St. Francis of Assisi called his body "Brother Ass."

The way begins with simple honesty (which leads to freedom). In this honest position, we see that we are unable, in ourselves, to conquer and overcome. We open our ears to the One who *is* able to overcome. We open our spirits to the indwelling of the Holy Spirit, the power source. We eat strengthening food: the word of God. It works in us to bring forth its own fruits. We pray as sons who have a relationship, who can rightfully expect an inheritance.

8 Taking Counsel

. . . What king, when he sets out to meet another king in battle, will not sit down first and take counsel whether he is strong enough with ten thousand to encounter the one coming against him with twenty thousand? Luke 14:31

Enlistment in any army is a contract, mutual promises between parties. The next chapter will bring us to the "Prayer of Agreement" that I found helpful in releasing God's power. This prayer constitutes a promise to God, who has already given His promises to us. Proverbs 20:25 says; "It is foolish and rash to make a promise to the Lord before counting the cost" (LB). This chapter will be a counting chapter, or "taking counsel" to see if you are ready for success.

Our enemy comes against us from two directions. The enemy within takes advantage of the weakness of our flesh. The enemy without allures and tempts through the world around us, and even sometimes through friends and family! These temptations will sometimes be so subtle as to seem diabolically planned (they are).

If we started by looking at the power and subtlety of our enemy, we would surely grow fainthearted, for the enemy is more powerful than we are. But we launch our counterattack from our position in Christ; anything less is doomed to fail. The Word says we are priests (Rev. 1:6). We hold this position by right of inheritance from our High Priest, who triumphed over principalities and powers, making a show of them openly, and now sitting in the seat of authority in heavenly places (Col. 2:15; Eph. 1:20).

Before I was ready for victory, I had to honestly expose some of my fears and neuroses so I could see them for what they were and accept God's healing power. We cannot treat fears and neuroses at length here; for one thing, I am not qualified, and for another, there wouldn't be room! I am familiar with some of the fears that beset fat people, and I learned that God has a healing process for them. Some of you will have already dealt with emotional problems, but others will need counsel to prepare for the battle.

God spoke to me when I was finally ready to hear. He said, "Joan, you have something else to lose that is ugly besides fat. Make your path straight before me, come to the end of your crooked path. . . ." I found that the other "ugly thing" God spoke of was many things all rolled into one—wow, were they rolled!

One of my doctors had given me a clue: I was not ready to be thin. Ask yourself, "Am I *afraid* to be thin?" What a dumb question! (That's what I thought. Look at all I've done to be thin—exercised, starved, suffered pills, shots, girdles—of course I'm not afraid to be thin!) And yet, some of us do have an unconscious fear of being thin. Psychiatrist Theodore I. Rubin, in *Forever Thin*, mentions that during analysis it is interesting to note how many overweight patients see thinness as an automatic conferring of beauty and irresistible sex appeal.

Married patients even fear this might incur adultery. Rubin's patients are often unhappy in their marriages, but afraid to admit that they themselves are the source of their unhappiness. Although they find fault with their mates, they are dependent on them and fearful of upsetting the status quo.

Admit your fears to God, and let Him show you by His Spirit how unreal it is to think that when you lose weight you will "automatically" get involved with things you shouldn't. God had to show this to *me*. When I took that idea out into the light of day, I realized that all around me were thin people who were normal, moral, and joyous; I just hadn't looked before. God's word told me things like this: "There is no fear in love," and the Holy Spirit helped me accept the truth and make it *mine*. Gradually God released me from the fear of being thin.

Genophobia is the technical word for fear of sex. Note that it is a "phobia" which is an "exaggerated and often disabling fear" (Webster). One woman who had lost eighty pounds told me she'd always been secretly fearful she might become a prostitute if she were thin; after losing weight, she realized how ridiculous this fear had been. It was, in fact, not so much a genuine fear as a flimsy excuse for imprisoning herself in a wall of fat, but she had never actually coped with it before.

Some people are afraid they won't be able to stop losing weight and will become emaciated! We fool no one but ourselves with such notions. When we lose weight, we do not lose the fat cells; we merely lose the fluid they contain. They lie there waiting to be filled up again. Nasty little things, aren't they? They are a major reason why diets don't work. Only a new life style will keep us thin. A few people go on unsafe diets so deficient in nutrients that they become ill. The zealots who follow such fads don't learn a thing about proper eating, and they endanger their lives.

You might be afraid that your husband won't like you thin.

Now, there could be some truth in this. It depends on your husband and you. Some people do feel "safer" with a fat spouse. Usually that is because they are insecure, and this will require reassurance from you and the Lord. Pray about this one.

One wife told me she was glad her husband was fat, because the girls liked him when he was not. Maybe he was afraid of being thin, or maybe she was the one who was afraid and cooked him right into her little prison, I don't know. But exchanging one sin for another is not what the Christian life is all about. An alcoholic shouldn't go on heroin because drunkenness gives him so much trouble!

A few wives are actually glad their husbands are in prisons—real ones—because they can't trust them when they're free. This is what the lady above wanted: a prison of fat. But if she truly loved her husband, she would want what was best for *him*, not for her. And if she truly loved him, chances are you couldn't have pried him away with a crowbar, he would have stuck around for the sheer joy of being loved.

Husbands and wives should want what is best for each other. And this includes support when one or the other is watching food intake. Don't eat forbidden foods in front of your partner. Care more for the other person than you do for yourself, and your marriage will be a sweet-smelling savor unto the Lord. (The obligation goes two ways: the "watcher" should not slip behind the other's back to gorge unseen. We answer to the Lord for the things done in our bodies.) If you are both on the same team and believe the victory announcement, you will act as unto the Lord. It will be a complete marriage instead of a "compete" marriage. If need be, reassure your partner that he doesn't have to keep you fat to keep you.

Another problem area is "role playing." We are accustomed to a certain role with our friends and family, and many fatties are afraid to lose weight because it means they can no longer fit the part they've played for years. It's true that a few people may no longer feel comfortable around you when you're thin. Part of my own healing was to discover that I had always unconsciously placed myself next to someone bigger than myself, in choir for instance, because it gave me some small measure of comfort to be around someone bigger than me!

Another fear may be losing friends. I used to subconsciously keep at least one friend who liked to eat as much as I did. I couldn't stand to go to lunch with someone who ate sparingly; it made me uncomfortable. (Some of your friends may like you for the same reason.) As an overcomer, you will be able to go to lunch with friends for true reasons: conversation, sharing, "edifying one another in love." Your real friends love your spirit, not your flesh, and will love you fat or thin.

Frequently the fattie of the family is the center of attention. He is urged "please go on a diet," "if you lose weight, I'll buy you a new wardrobe," and so forth. This is a comfortable role, and you may be afraid of losing it. The emotional part of our problem is a factor here. Some family members or friends will say they want you thin, but their actions will prove differently. They may offer you tempting desserts, or eat them in front of you. Some folks are just opposed to change, even when it's for the better! They may get some unrecognized satisfaction in comparing themselves with you. This is psychological dependence, and for all the wrong reasons. Don't blame these people; they haven't really understood what was going on. As you mature and become thin, you will not need these mutual-backscratching friendships. You will be free to build true friendships.

One of the reasons I ate goodies compulsively was because there were four kids in my family (the real one) and I thought I had to cram it all in now as there might not be any left later.

39

Most of us—fat or thin—are afraid that we'll starve, or that we won't get our "fair share." Our fair share gets larger and larger as we stretch our capacity. Finally we reach the stage where we're ashamed to eat all we can in public and we resort to secret eating.

Some fatties know a few things about what bugs them, but most of us don't go far enough. What makes me eat too much? Am I afraid of another economic depression? Am I afraid this will be my last meal? Am I afraid somebody else will get it? This shows where we are spiritually; God's word teaches us to be "anxious" for nothing, and to be generous, hospitable, and compassionate. It not only teaches us what we *should* be, when we read it carefully, it tells us *how* to be; it provides the model for restorative confession, repentance, and healing.

God caused the ravens to bring food to Elijah, and He fed the Israelites by raining down bread from heaven. If he did that today, the Baker's Union would object. While He was doing these things, He tried to show Israel that their real "meat" was to do the will of God. Jesus is the Bread of Life, and He feeds us so that we do not hunger. This is a gradual process, not the overnight magic that most of us wish for, but it is a "more sure way." Those of us who hunger for more than we need, for more than is good for us, have another hunger: we have emotional problems that we have not exposed to the healing of our Lord Jesus. Our hunger is really for something other than food, but we have accepted food as a substitute and programmed our "appestat" until we crave more food than we can use. But there is good news: the Holy Spirit can heal these unnamed hungers; our "excessive capacity problem" has a cure.

There are nearly as many fears as there are people. We cannot name them all, but we have identified the pattern. If we choose to reverse the path we've been traveling, to be honest before God and let Him heal, to accept His power to overcome, we're on the road.

Jesus has another gift that casts out fear: Love. Even fat people experience a weight loss when they fall in love! We can never really learn to know Jesus from other people. The Holy Spirit reveals Him to us as we read His word, and we will find ourselves falling in love! It begins with a decision to abide in His word, as He commanded, and it leads to the ecstasy of the bride for the bridegroom, which Jesus calls His relationship with those who truly love Him. Jesus asks the bride to prepare herself for His coming. True, He wasn't referring to our earthly bodies; He *was* referring to our spiritual welfare. God is not concerned about our size, but He is concerned about obedience. He wants us to have the fruit of the Spirit, including self-control. And lovers always want to do what the loved one asks.

When the Lord first introduced the word "rebellion" to me, I protested, "Who, me, Lord? I'm not rebellious, I'm a lover!" (Sure, a lover of food.) God has said that we can't serve two masters; we will love the one and hate the other (Matt. 6:24). Food is a cruel master, and demands complete service. We say we hate it, but our flesh loves it.

There was a time when I said I'd do anything if only I could be thin, like cut off my right arm. . . . I've made some rash statements about what I'd give up to be thin, which is funny considering that I had to give up only one thing: food addiction. If I'd been honest, I'd have said, "Take away anything, God, except my food," which is a neat little insult to God, inferring that the things He gave me, like arms and legs, were less important than food. I had despised God's goodness and set up an idol!

When I talk about rebellion, I'm talking about something I know about. I was one of the "3R" girls: rotten, rebellious, rough. When I confessed my rebellion and repented of it, God took my heart of stone and exchanged it for a heart of flesh. Denying that we are rebellious when we have obvious evidence of it is a waste of time. Confession and repentance brings healing, and when God does the healing, it is done right, from the inside out, a complete work. The anger, the cheated feelings, the fear that we won't get our share will drop away, and we will hardly notice their passing, for God will be filling the void with joy, maturity, and satisfaction.

If you find, when you examine yourself, that you are not quite ready and willing to let God begin His work in you, set your mind to be willing to be made willing. This is the place of commitment. God can work beneath the conscious level to bring you to the place of willingness. Trust the matter into His hands. Every time you think of it, pray "I've already turned the matter over to you, Lord. Thank you for taking care of it." Rest in the knowledge that God will perform as promised. One day you will discover that your attitude, your "wanter," has changed. Then you can set your mind on the goal that lines up with God's word, and He can take you there.

Righteousness is obedience to God, putting Him first. He has promised that righteousness yields "peaceful fruit." We will be at peace when we have ceased battling for our own willful, rebellious way. Yielding to God's way requires discipline, but you will discover that the promise is true: there is a power source that will help you even with the discipline. When you have determined to glorify God in your body, you have set your course, for the battleground is in the mind.

We have been eating food to satisfy a deep need, and it never will. Only spiritual food will satisfy that craving. "Say there, is anyone thirsty? Come and drink, even if you have no money. Come and take your choice of wine and milk; it's all free. Why spend your money on foodstuffs that don't do you any good? Listen and I'll tell you where to get good food that fattens up the soul" (Isa. 55:1 LB).

There's the problem and the solution. We fed an undernourished soul with the wrong food, and ended with a fat body instead of a fat soul. The soul kept craving, and we kept feeding it wrong food. But we're learning the big secret: When we fatten our souls, our bodies will become thinner and stay that way. We can satisfy the "new man" with everlasting food, and our eating pattern will get into the right perspective: food for living rather than living for food.

9 A Word in Season

A man hath joy in the answer of his mouth; and a word in due season how good it is. Proverbs 15:23

After trying every way I heard of to lose weight and finding myself a flop at all of them, I was desperate enough to try almost anything. Fortunately, I tried the Prayer of Agreement, which turned the key to the right door. This prayer is a promise to the Lord, but it is more than that: it is a decision of the will backed by the power of prayer and the power of agreement. It is getting down to business, the starting line on the road to self-control. I wrote out my pledge and committed myself to accept God's help and guidance. I can almost hear someone exclaiming, "What, don't tell me this silly woman is going to ask me to sign a piece of paper and *that* is going to make the difference!"

Whoa, there! It involves more than that. Promises to God are not to be taken lightly. In the past we have had good intentions, we have even made promises, and broken them all.

Giving our word lightly is a sin that grieves the Lord God; this time we will counsel together in His word and appropriate strength from God himself to be able to give a true word.

Our own word gets shot full of holes because there is an enemy with a quiver full of arrows. "Big Red" is hanging around to see who he can catch making "fat mistakes," and his strength is greater than ours—when we stand alone. James tells us not to "swear by" anything, because a vow taken on the strength of our word alone won't cut it. If you're standing on your word alone, you had better look down, because that is the direction you will soon be traveling! Malachi 2:17 gives a picture of a man's word when he stands alone: "You have wearied the Lord with your words. Wearied him? you ask in fake surprise, how have we wearied him? By saying that evil is good, that it pleases the Lord, or by saying that 'God won't punish us, he doesn't care.' " The Israelites were famous for forsaking the counsel of God and going their own self-reliant way. They were also famous for their failures!

I am amazed at the number of plump people who ask me how I lost weight, and when I tell them, they break in to tell me why that couldn't work for them, and what *will* work—in spite of the evidence to the contrary! I shouldn't be too surprised, for I am familiar with the way fatties shield themselves from the truth with rationalizations and excuses and farfetched ideas, so when this happens, I ask God for grace to wait. Our thinking is fuzzy when we are overweight, and Satan, our enemy, likes for us to keep our illusions and does everything he can to deceive. You will make a leap forward when you are ready to forsake your own words and seek the good words of God.

The starting place is to *hear* those good words. There's a saying that when a kid is five he has all the questions, and at fifteen he has all the answers. At twenty he may be getting ready to hear what other people say. I was amazed at how smart my parents got in the five years when I grew from fifteen to

A Word in Season

twenty. At fifteen I did the talking and at twenty I was finally
ready to listen. At thirty, the Lord taught me the value of not
only listening, but *hearing*. The scriptural meaning of hearing
is that you are ready to *act* on what you hear. Jesus sorrowed for
eyes that saw but did not see, for ears that heard but did not
hear. How about the death of Lazarus, or the obstinacy of
Jerusalem? If you have remnants of self-sufficiency, you are
still trying to rely on yourself, and you may not be ready to hear
and act. If this is the case, I hope you keep this book and try
again. If you are not sure that you are ready to take this step, try
recalling the methods you've used so far to lose weight: diets,
pills, shots, hypnosis, psychiatry, exercise, reducing belts,
fasting, surgery, and all the rest. Now recall how many of these
worked with lasting results. Then admit you don't have the
answer, and if you can agree that it's time to quit talking and
start hearing, you are ready to sign up in the Overcomer's
Army. And I shout *Welcome*, for you are in the right place; you
are ready to run with the Winners!

The winners are the ones who have run the race and received
the prize. Paul gives us the clue and the encouragement: "Do
you know that those who run in a race all run, but only one
receives the prize? Run in such a way that you may win, and
everyone who competes in the games exercises self-control in
all things. They do it to receive a perishable wreath, but we an
imperishable" (I. Cor. 9:23-27). The world exercises self-
control for a mere perishable prize! How much more is offered
to us: a crown for all eternity. And further, we have a special
source of help, a Creator who is keenly interested in our
receiving the prize. He has provided the training manual, and
He didn't stop there; He offers strength to us by the power of
His own Holy Spirit. *His strength is imparted to our weakness*
(see II Cor. 12:9). With a combination like that, the weakest
person can be a winner. Giving our word is so serious that we
might tremble and never give it at all except for this "weight of

glory" that God makes available to us. If God asks it, we can do it, because He provides the way—His strength, by His word.

If we have been failure oriented because His promises didn't seem to work for us in the past, we will have to face the fact that the failure was *ours*, not His. We did not accept the keys that He handed us. God is *for* us; He is not trying to trick or trap us. He is interested in us, not just for the future in eternity, but *now*. He cares about the things done in our bodies, and because this is so we can bring all the power of heaven into our daily lives. "And I will give you the keys of the kingdom of heaven; whatever doors you open on earth shall be opened in heaven, and whatever doors you lock on earth shall be locked in heaven" (Matt. 16:19).

God is the one who asks us to glorify Him in our bodies, and He is the one who gives us the power to do it: "All things are lawful for me, but I will not be mastered by anything. Food is for the stomach, and the stomach is for food; but God will do away with both of them. Yet the body is not for immorality, but for the Lord; and the Lord is for the body. Now God has not only raised the Lord, but will also raise us up through His power. . . . Or do you not know that your body is a temple of the Holy Spirit who is in you, whom you have from God, and that you are not your own? For you have been bought with a price: therefore, glorify God in your body" (I. Cor. 6:12b, 13-14, 19-20). Now we have already determined that alone we can do nothing, but we can do "all things through Christ, who strengthens me, which the Father asketh of me" (Phil. 4:13).

There is a difference between our word and God's word: His is a sure thing! His word is always in due season, and it is good, the right place to begin. Then when we are ready to speak, our word will have taken on the character of His word. This "divine osmosis" is one of the secrets and mysteries of the Christian life. We can't always explain it, but we can benefit by it!

We have often said "I'm going to do this or that," and then we did the opposite. One reason is that we begin with "I." Silence would be better than such rash promises. "The man of few words and settled mind is wise, therefore, even a fool is thought to be wise when he is silent" (Prov. 17:27-28). This is not the time for rash promises; this is the time to settle our minds through the use of God's word, then when we speak we will need only a few words. It is not the "words" that we speak that do the job; it is the "settled mind," the *decision of the will*.

Nothing we have said or can say in this book about overcoming is any good without a decision of the will. A decision has power. We step from slavery into a kingdom by a decision. We pass from death into life by a decision. Emotions may accompany our decisions, but the real work is accomplished by the decision. It will work for you when you decide to be an overcomer by the power of God. This powerful force begins deep inside us and heals from the inside out. It is done by faith, believing that God hears and accepts it. It is done in the name of Jesus, for there is power in that name (John 16:23). Setting the will to accept God's two-way offer will work, because the work is done by God, the dependable party in this agreement.

When we are born anew, we make a decision and God responds with a gift of repentance. We accept this gift by "performing it"—by acting it out, or repenting. He responds with His promised forgiveness and reconciliation. We then stand on this transaction by faith, as He instructs us to do; the "treaty" has been ratified by both parties. "Now, being justified by faith, you have peace with God through our Lord and Saviour Jesus Christ" (Rom. 5:1). It is a sure, dependable transaction with certified results. The same process works for spiritual growth, for overcoming. You start with a decision of the will. God will show you the sin that defeated you, and you confess it as a sin against Him. He will give you a spirit of repentance, and again, you accept His gift by repenting.

Repentance is such an integral part of God's scheme that we

cannot expect to be either Christians or Christian overcomers without it! Webster says that the word "repent" means to feel sorrow or regret for a sin, to change your mind about it, to show penitence by turning from it, to abandon it, and to dedicate oneself to the amendment of your life! This is a tall order and we might have trouble fulfilling it except that it, too, is a gift of God. If He sees a settled mind He will respond as promised. This act of obedience is effective and powerful, and you will experience the peace of God and His healing power.

In the past, we have taken food as a substitute "comforter" instead of the one God provided, the Holy Spirit. We have despised God's gift and set up an idol. When we repent of this rebellion and idolatry, we will have started a process that has a predictable outcome: we will be overcomers by the power of God. We will not have a lifelong struggle because the new man has been given the freedom to react as his heavenly Father directs. Our "wanters" will be changed. Result: deliverance and victory by the power of God.

The Prayer of Agreement was the first thing I tried that had a permanent effect on my problem. Because I was so well aware of my old weakness, I was willing to write up the "contract" whereby the terms of my pact with God were specified, giving me the decision of a "settled mind." God didn't need to see my name on a dotted line—but I did! I had made so many promises and forgotten them the next day, that I was willing to do anything that would help this one "take." That's why I asked my husband to agree with me in this covenant. "If two of you agree down here on earth concerning anything you ask for, my Father in heaven will do it for you, for where two or three gather together because they are mine, I will be right there among them" (Matt. 18:19).

The Prayer of Agreement has power behind it because God has said it. All this power is waiting to be tapped by people, including fat ones! If you don't realize how much power there is in agreement, take a look at Ananias and Sapphira. They made an agreement to deceive, and the power of their agreement was so strong they ended up dead. The same power is available for life. Agreement before God for righteousness is life-giving.

I assure you that I did not come out on top every single day. But failure can't change a decision. We don't let our failures force us to quit being Christians. No! We ask forgiveness, pick up our weary knees, and dance to the tune "Jesus is the rock of my salvation." So after every failure I pick myself up and keep going. I have given my word, and God is keeping His. I had a contract with God, and He was more interested in my attaining the goal than in my never having a failure!

Even the world recognizes "love pledges" as valid; this is what we do when we get married. Once taken, these promises are binding. Although marriage vows do not command the respect they once did, the law of our land still fines you heavily if you want to cancel them! They put a price on them. Believe me, once you have entered into a love contract with God and felt His power flowing back to you, you will think the arrangement is above price. God always gives back more than He asks of us!

The Christian life seems "foolish" to the world. The Christian has staked his life on a concept: that there is a God who created us, as evidenced by nature, our own conscience, and the Word; and this God requires something of us. He requires a yielded heart, a firm decision of the will to forsake the world and follow after the One who is revealed to us by the Holy Spirit. Our affirmative decision is an agreement that God's word is true. As we learn of Him, we find that there is a power source at our disposal, a whole basketful of promises that will work for us if we fit ourselves into His word as He asks. His word has specific instructions to the one who wants to attain abundant life, the prize of our high calling, which amounts to overcoming the world, the flesh, and the devil! We tap our power source by feeding on it: through prayer and the written word we fellowship with the One who is powerful! When we have settled our minds to accept the abundant life that God offers, we will be drawn to the word that instructs, strengthens, and sets us free!

The Prayer of Agreement is the easiest way to be an overcomer that has ever been known. Decision from within and power from without, with two in agreement to tap all the power of God: a winning combination for those ready to be winners.

Find a quiet time and place. If you can't find one, make one! We can be victors rather than victims by the simple act of taking command of our time and our lazy selves. The process will grow easier with practice, but you may have to take a deep breath and jump in to get started. Once in your quiet place, level with God about your decision and let Him feed you from His word. Here is a suggestion: read I Cor. 6:12-20, I Cor. 9:24-27, I Cor. 10:5-15, especially verse 13. Then, write your contract in your own handwriting and make it yours alone. When you have signed it, get your agreement partner to sign it. If it makes you feel silly to ask someone to share it with you, remember Naaman who thought that dipping in the river seven times sounded silly, but when he was persuaded to try it, he was glad he did! He was cured of leprosy. I was not *eager* to enter into this contract with God, but I was willing—I had no one else to turn to. Obedience was all that was left. Our weakness has been so very evident; this step will make our obedience evident, too!

Here is a sample of the agreement I made with God; feel free to change it to fit your personality.

This agreement is made with the living God on _____(date). My intent is to shut the door on my past sin of gluttony and open the door to my healing. I claim God's wisdom and power to overcome the tempter. I know my Father expects me to use the weapon of His word, and if I lose one battle,* I will still claim His strength to win the war over gluttony.

I claim Gal. 5:22 for my self-control, as part of my inheritance as a child of God. I agree to resist the devil as instructed in James 4:7 so that he will flee from me. I agree to eat freely of God's word so that it may abide in me and my prayers will be answered.

My eating plan is _____
(can be named here and a copy attached)

Satan, in the name of Jesus, my partner and I notify you that according to this agreement you are bound on this day and hour, and we render you helpless in this matter. You will not function, operate, harass, embarrass, or in any other way intimidate these agreement partners, because this pact is made in the name of the Lord Jesus Christ who came to earth in the flesh to put to death your deeds and rose from the grave victorious.

My agreement partner has read this contract and agrees with me for my victory. He/She agrees to support me in prayer and in action. In keeping with Matt. 18:19-20, we claim together that victory is ours over intemperance, agreeing in the name of Jesus according to John 16:23.

Signed _____

Signed _____

---

* Formulas don't work by themselves. It's the relationship we have with Jesus that counts. Call on him, first. He healed crippled people before he told them to walk—although it was often nearly simultaneous.

10 And With Your Wisdom...

Develop common sense and good judgment.

Wisdom requires a decision. "Determination to be wise is the first step toward becoming wise. And with your wisdom, develop common sense and good judgment" (Prov. 5:7). This is a scriptural pattern: decision, then development. We fatties seem always to want an overnight miracle, a magic potion, anything that doesn't require any effort on our part. (We're not the only ones; that's what a lot of people want.) There's no way to get magic, but there is a promise that the effort you put forth *will be rewarded with success* because God's pattern develops the components of success: common sense and good judgment.

Not only can we acquire wisdom, we can have it in plenty. "If any of you lack wisdom, let him ask of God and it shall be liberally given to you" (James 1:5). We have perhaps asked God for wisdom in the past; if it didn't happen, it was because we asked amiss. The Bible says that we ask amiss when our intent is to consume it upon our own lusts. We wanted to have our wisdom and our eating too. We also ask amiss when we do not *accept* the gift from the hand of God. His gifts are accepted by using them. Since the particular gift we are asking for involves our behavior, acceptance means acting it out. If we believe God, we will start acting like it!

If our understanding has been dulled by inattention in the past, God has a further gift: *The Holy Spirit will teach us* (John 16:13). Reading carefully and prayerfully allows Him to teach it as you go. The light will begin to shine, and you will become conscious of the unseen but powerful force that is the Christian secret: all things are possible through the One who imparts Himself to us.

We overeaters tend to ask for wisdom about eating *after* we have eaten; we want to get comfortable first! Our first act of wisdom should be to claim God's help before we eat. We need to fill our minds with the good words of God so we can apply what He says directly to our problem. God's word is wisdom, and the application of it develops common sense and good judgment.

The word has an effect: it washes and cleanses our minds (Titus 3:5, John 15:3), and the daily teaching applied by the Holy Spirit leads to maturity (John 14:26, I John 2:27). When these processes of truth and healing take place, the yield is *joy*. "These things have I spoken unto you . . . that your joy might be full" (John 15:11).

The reason we can be so sure of the results is because the Creator has made us in a divine pattern: the image of God. When we follow his instructions, we can depend on the results! We were created to *know* God and to *enjoy* Him forever, which means we have been "pre-set" to respond. When we begin to eat of His goodness, we will develop a taste for His words. The psalmist sang, "Sweet are thy words to my mouth, sweeter than the honeycomb . . ." (Psalm 119:103), and this is how it will be when our taste buds have developed. It may take discipline while the old craving is stronger than the new, but it will come; we can count on it.

Here's another discipline that falls under the heading of wisdom: don't *talk* a lot about your new eating plan. People get sick of listening to a lot of diet talk and all our problems, the reasons we can't get thin, and the reasons why we fail. Be content to wait and let them notice the change, then you can tell them about the spiritual change that has taken place, which is more important anyway. There is some strange correlation between talking too much and doing too little. It seems that we satisfy ourselves by talking so much, the conscience is coated over, and we don't have to *act*. So discipline yourself not to talk about it, and concentrate on *doing* what you have purposed and pledged to do.

Our real problems are deeply rooted. They require superior wisdom and power to overcome them. I was a time-waster. I lived by compulsions—eating, watching TV, cooking, talking on the phone, and spending money with gusto whenever the mood struck me. Once I started a job, I was driven to finish it, but my moods, like lightning, never struck twice in the same place. And so I was an utterly unorganized housekeeper.

Many overweight people are people-pleasers. They want to feel needed and important—they want other people to think they're wonderful—so they never say no. They do things for people that they wouldn't do for themselves and, as a result, they don't have enough energy left to plan, shop, and cook properly for health and weight control.

If people-pleasing causes you to neglect yourself, you will need to stop the merry-go-round and take time to learn the art of overcoming. It will take wisdom and discernment to recognize the enemy, "time-eater." But a little common sense and good judgment will work wonders. Remember, you will be more valuable to everyone when you have gained the mastery of self-control. Our Lord recognized the value of having time to himself. He went to the desert. Paul spent three years on the desert before he began his ministry, and Moses spent forty years on the desert. So declare a time of "preparation on the desert" and brace yourself to break the pattern of time-wasting, whether for yourself or others. Our enemy would like to make us feel selfish for taking the time for planning, study, or even resting.

All of the things we have been talking about—study of God's word, planning for proper eating and care of oneself—fall under the heading of discipline. Those of us who have had a weakness for food are obviously not well-disciplined, so we need reproof from God's word. "Whoever loves discipline loves knowledge, but he who hates reproof is stupid" (Prov. 12:1). That's laying it on the line! If we are wise, we will love discipline; it's that simple.

Discipline in God's word yields spiritual development, and spiritual growth has a tangible payoff. Overeaters like to have plenty of food squirreled away—in the stomach, in the refrigerator, in the cupboard. Let any one of these show empty space, and we panic. God had a plan for breaking the Israelites of this dependency on their storage facilities. "People shall go out and gather a day's portion every day, that I may prove them, whether they will walk in my law or not . . ." (Exo. 16:4). He clamped down on their resources to show them that they could trust Him. (This will show up rebellion in a hurry!)

Here is an important point: the flesh tends to squirrelishness; the spirit trusts God. Since, as the Bible says, the flesh cannot please God, we must develop the spirit, and the payoff of spiritual development will be trust. God programmed squirrels to store up food for the winter, but He programmed people to trust Him. A squirrel with his mouth full of nuts has puffy cheeks, and people who have given their stomachs over to squirrelishness have puffy everything. God went to great lengths to prove to man that He is capable of taking care of tomorrow. Learning trust will change a basic attitude that has defeated us. We will "get off the ground" and leave behind the earthbound squirrels who have to store up their share. We will get up there with the carefree birds who fly through heavenly places to spend winter in the south.

King Solomon, that wise man with a fondness for the fair sex, portrays both wisdom and folly as women who sit in their doorways and call to men to come eat at their tables (a sure way to catch them). The lady Wisdom has furnished her house and set her table, and she sends her maidens out to call, "Whoso is simple [easily led astray, wavering], let him turn in here! . . . He that lacks understanding, come, eat of my bread and drink of the wine I have mingled; forsake the foolish ways and live, and go in the way of understanding." We fatties have lacked understanding of our problem, but here we are offered the bread and wine of wisdom which give life. It isn't like us to turn down a dinner invitation; we have only to make sure we choose the right one!

In contrast to this invitation is another from the woman Folly. She also sits in her doorway, but she has not prepared her table with good food—she plans to steal it! She calls to the same people: "Whoso is simple, let him turn in here, and he that wants understanding . . . well, stolen waters are sweet, and bread eaten in secret is pleasant." Stolen pleasures and secret eating . . . do we not know what she's talking about? Sounds like she's calling to overeaters. Come, eat! Steal it if you must, be sneaky if you can, be anything at all, but by all means be full! But there is a catch: hers is the doorway to the dead, and her guests are in the depths of hell! She is noisy, forward, and open to all forms of evil (Prov. 9:13).

If this sounds like a story you've never heard before, you can

59

read all about it in Proverbs, ninth chapter. (Maybe we've taken just a little liberty to apply it to our problem, but not much; it's all there.) The key to the passage is in verse 8: "Rebuke a wise man, and he will love thee." Dear overweight reader, let us accept the right invitation and go to the feast of the lady Wisdom. Eating from her table is the way of life and understanding. Those stolen nibbles and the bread eaten in secret have been our undoing! "We have eaten, and not been satisfied, and there's still hunger in our inward parts" (see Micah 6:14). We were at the wrong table.

God's word began to heal my "decision maker." Little by little, I faced decisions in the kitchen, at the table, at the store. The bakery truck was the first to go, and my shopping and cooking habits began to change. My imagination had to be stirred to think of good salads and vegetable dishes and my lazy body had to be prodded to learn new ways. But there was a "weight of glory" along the way. I asked God to give me delight in the good foods that He had provided and to help me "do all things as unto the Lord" in preparing new foods. As the pounds went, energy improved so that I did not notice the extra work and, in time, I had energy to spare. The word of God has a way of healing our emotional conflicts, which also have drained our energy. As I learned to apply the word of God to my wounded psyche, I began to heal. God is a God of plenty; I didn't have to be a squirrel. It took some time, but there was a change.

The best news of all is that we don't have to wait until we succeed to enter the exciting life of an overcomer. God has a way of ministering blessings along the way. When Jesus resisted Satan, he left, and the angels came and ministered to Jesus. God will do the same for you. An angel is a messenger, and God uses all kinds of messengers to minister His blessings. You will receive a phone call, a letter, a word in season from your pastor or a friend, or best of all, an infusion of comfort and strength from God's word through His Holy Spirit. So resist the tempter with the power of God's word, and get ready to be ministered to!

11 Where the Action Is

Changing our habits is where we enter combat. We find how badly we have trained our flesh, and we meet the foe; but, *We are not ignorant of his devices.* II Corinthians 2:11

The nitty-gritty of daily combat can get pretty earthy. One of Satan's cleverest ruses is to help us be "religious" so we will leave Christ out of our practical, day-to-day lives. But Jesus walked on dusty roads and sweated under the Palestine sun. He hungered and thirsted and talked to Samaritans. He didn't hesitate to bring the lofty principles and precepts of God into the daily battle, and He set a lot of "religious" folk's teeth on edge!

Christ "drew fire," and you are going to draw it too when you start walking contrary to the "prince of this world." Until now, you have had a sort of truce with the enemy of your soul, but when you pull down the white flag and take up weapons, he is going to start fighting. Conquering my flesh proved to be a real battleground. Correction: a war. To give the devil his due, I must admit that I had played into his hands for so long that he had some reason to think I didn't mean it when I told him he was defeated. And yet—this time—I was able to win the war. This time, when I drew fire I was wearing armor.

The very first skirmish is called "*Now.*" We want to put off subduing the flesh until later. I had plenty of trouble getting started. After I had given in to the flesh, remorse would set in. I would moan, "You fat slob, you can never have the victory. You will never, never overcome like other people; you are hooked on food forever." But the other voice wouldn't let me go. Christ has won the victory. "I can do all things through Christ which strengthens me" (Phil. 4:13).

Your head, which has been in conspiracy with your flesh, will tell you that you are defeated, but your heart, where you have sown the seed of the word of God, knows you're not! Listen to your heart. God's thoughts are higher than man's thoughts. As we input the word of God, we are sowing the things we lack, and they will take root and grow (all they need is continued watering).

God delights in taking a weak, unsteady man and making something of him! His plan is unique. We don't have to wait until we get better; in fact, we can't get better. We don't have to achieve a certain goal before we can be rewarded; His plan is to help us achieve!

The secret is the "input." Without it we can do nothing; with it we can do everything. Begin inputting, and God will take care of the increase, or, in our case, the *decrease.* Spiritual input = fat spirit = victory over the flesh = smaller bodies. Believe it. The last chapter of this book is devoted to spiritual input, and it is the most important chapter in the book. There is a way to build your strength: put on Christ Jesus.

The next bad habit we need to deal with is that old desire to lose all our excess overnight. We should know by now that it doesn't work that way, but fatties are famous for being gullible. The result of this attitude has always been the same: fat. What we need is a new life style. We already know what happens to quick-weight-loss diets—the diets go much quicker than the weight. The chapter dealing with food plan selection will stress choosing a plan that is right for you and realistic. The battle is not "Which food plan?" but rather "When do I overcome?"

The habit of thinking of our goal—the day the last pound is shed—has defeated us in the past. God is concerned with our victory *today*. In His eyes you are just as much an overcomer the *first day you overcome* as the last. The world may not see the first few pounds you lose, but God sees the victory and the renewing of the mind on the first day of our new life-plan as much as on the last; it's the *overcoming* that counts. Just plan to overcome one day at a time and let the weight loss be incidental.

The anxiety principle works here. God's word says "Be anxious for nothing." He knows that the more anxious we are, the less we get done. So He tells us to "cast all our care upon Him" and get on with the work at hand, which is to overcome on a daily basis. We are not out to set records in weight loss, but to glorify God in our bodies. And He is a God of common sense and sound judgment; He is more interested in the new *you* than in fast weight loss. So be firm when those anxieties rise before you, whether they take the form of pride and vanity, or of fear and defeat. Treat them alike: talk to God about them, tell Him you are unable to deal with them properly, and cast them on Him.

If you have an appetite that is so maladjusted that you have a wild craving for something you simply should not eat, pray for deliverance from that appetite. If the struggle gets particularly intense, begin crying out, "Jesus, help me, Jesus, help me!" I can promise you that as your body gets used to a more wholesome diet, it will begin to experience a satisfied feeling and lose its craving for strange foods.

The victory plan is a pattern of change. As we begin to break up the habit patterns that we have slipped into, we will discover a lot of things we didn't know about ourselves. One of my bad habits that I finally recognized was the simple one of looking into the refrigerator. I didn't always plan to eat something, but I looked anyway, just checking my security. The worst day of my life occurred six years ago (before victory), when the handle broke off the refrigerator. Suddenly my entire life seemed to depend on being able to look in to see how the food was doing. I acted like a paramedic giving mouth-to-mouth resuscitation to a dying friend; I used a screwdriver and hammer and finally succeeded in fixing it. Such a relief! And for what? So I could gaze upon my iniquity. A cartoon or Scripture verse (or both) pasted on the door of the fridge will help you break this habit.

My battle plan for habit-breaking left my kitchen looking a bit like the paste-up department in the city news room, with cartoons and Scripture verses posted on refrigerator and cupboard doors, inside and out, above the sink, and wherever else I needed them. There was a card file with Scripture verses on the table and notes to myself here and there. My attitude was that I would use anything that would help me translate my new decision and new truth into reality. My old habits were firmly entrenched, and I didn't see anything wrong with nailing up signposts all along the way to help me remember what I was doing.

Probably the worst habit we have—and the hardest to overcome—is the way we cook. I was horrified when I started facing the truth about myself to see what a lazy, dirty housekeeper I had become. My world had been reduced to eating and laying around as much as possible. Consequently my cooking pattern consisted of getting the most in quantity and rich calories with the least effort on my part. Unfortunately, the excess weight tended to laziness! My mind ran to easy casseroles where you opened six cans and dumped them together along with bread crumbs and cheese, passed them through the oven, and served them with a bakery cake and ice cream for dessert. Add some pickles and potato chips and you have the perfect formula for maximum weight gain and minimum energy.

Remember that ninety percent of your battle is going to be in your mind. After you have planned a sensible shopping list, have exercised discipline while shopping, and have cooked a nutritious meal with meat and lots of vegetables and a salad, *then* you are going to enjoy the food and find it's lots easier to eat properly. The trouble is, you will find that somebody is waiting for you all along this road to trip you up before you get there. We have an enemy, and he has designed his world to cater to our human weaknesses.

There is only one place to begin this battle: when you first wake up in the morning. That is the time for prayer and food from God's word. Put your day in the hands of God and renew your mind with good words from His book. Then, later, when you write out your shopping list, it will be relatively easy to keep your head on straight while you write out the foods that you will need for sensible eating.

The place for discipline will begin when you hit the aisles of the supermarket. Eating is a good and necessary function, but it has been perverted by an enemy into an invitation to indulgence and disaster. The world provides ready-made gluttony specials on every hand. The Bible says that in the last days there will be eating and drinking as in the days of Noah, and that day is here! Everywhere I look I see fat Christians, and fat non-Christians too. I think Satan has a special bag of dirty tricks for fat Christians, because he has them right where he wants them and plans to keep them there. He loved to see me stuff my face and make food my god. As your "wanter" changes, you will see through the advertising gimmicks, and the non-nutritious stuffers won't look as good any more. But right at first you are going to have to pretend you are on a real battlefield and the enemy is lying in wait to ambush you behind every stack of ready-made starchy stuffers. There were some aisles of the store I wouldn't even walk down!

In essence, our enemies are three: the world, the flesh, and the devil, just like the Bible says. As for the world, remember that Madison Avenue is no friend of yours. Satan controls the world, and the devices he employs to bait his tempter's snare are beautiful on the outside—but look out; there's a fishhook inside. As you dedicate yourself to the creator of the world and the one who is the true prince and victor, you will begin to discern the difference between the good, natural foods that God created for your good health and enjoyment and the snacky stuff that the world offers as a deadly substitute. It may not be deadly when taken in moderation, but to those of us who are susceptible, it sets up its own craving within us and we are "hooked." We overeaters are in the same boat as alcoholics; we have a susceptibility to overindulgence. The second enemy, our poorly-trained flesh, will clamor for things it should not have, but it is going to be overcome by the Spirit of God as we strengthen it from God's word. The third enemy, the "old man" himself, requires a close look.

Satan will use every trick in his nasty little book. He knows us "like a book" and he will use all he knows. But we have a better book, and it provides us with a resume of this tempter! God gave us down-to-earth knowledge of Satan to prepare us for the daily action.

Satan is a hinderer: "Wherefore we would have come to you, even I Paul, once and again, but Satan hindered us" (I Thess. 2:18). There is a cure for hindrance: resistance. "Resist the devil and he will flee from you" (James 4:7). Satan is also a devourer, roaring like a lion to scare us (I Pet. 5:8), but when we take refuge in Jesus, he is only a lion with all his teeth removed. He may roar, but his "bark is worse than his bite." Jesus is the true lion, the lion of the Tribe of Judah, and He is our defense.

Satan has another role: he is a tempter. "For this reason when I could bear it no longer, I sent that I might know your faith, for fear that the tempter had tempted you and that our labor would be in vain" (I Thess. 3:5). But if you are walking with God, He "will not allow you to be tempted more than you are able to resist" (I Cor. 10:13). If this sounds on the surface like some "quick answers" to an easy combat, let me assure you, that is not the case! These answers are given to reassure us that there is an answer and that it will appear in due time; but in between there can be quite a battle! There is no getting around the fact that when we go against the current that we have been swimming with, we will feel all the power of the enemy.

The greed and indulgence that formed our life (and much of the life of the world!) has become a tide, a force or power that sweeps us along. We would be helpless in its grip, except . . . except that our God has provided us with a counterforce. Our decision was a powerful force, and our acceptance of God's strength will carry that force to its end. We have prepared ourselves with counsel and wisdom from without, and we have begun to armor ourselves from God's word, the sword of the Spirit. Our success as overcomers now depends on our "footwork" when confronted with our weakness: excess food. It is our temptation, and Satan will use it against us. Fortunately, there are ways to improve our footwork.

Modern boxers improve their techniques by replaying movies of former fights. They study their past mistakes and the tactics of their opponents. We can do this, too, for we have been furnished several "reels" of former action. One of these reels is that famous Garden Scene, which can give us some clues.

Eve was "tempted" through deception. Satan trapped her into coveting the forbidden food, then deceived her into thinking nothing would happen if she ate it. He stirred her curiosity by implying that God had some delicious secret that He wanted to keep from her. Note how Satan "tantalizes." Then he started "reasoning" with Eve: God hadn't really meant what He said . . . no harm would come to her! You will soon learn to catch yourself when you are tantalized followed by Satan's reasoning.

Women are still tempted with food. In one way or another, their lives seem to be consumed by it. Think of the number of women who are on a diet, have been on one, or are going on one tomorrow. Think of the time spent on food, thinking of it, buying it, cooking it, eating it, cleaning up after it, and talking about it, whether you eat or whether you diet! Most of our men would agree with the original Adam and say, "That woman you gave me, she did eat."

Adam's temptation wasn't the eating; he was drawn to Eve. He didn't want to lose her. He was not deceived; his sin was disobedience and his temptation came through beautiful Eve. She made him happy, and he was used to her. He chose her above his obedience to God.

Men are living a rerun of this famous movie to this day. Men spend almost as much time thinking of, looking for, and living for women as women spend on food. And both men and women try to excuse themselves and somehow escape the immutable laws of God.

So Eve desired food and Adam desired Eve. There were just the two of them, so what could possibly go wrong? They became separated, that's what went wrong. They no longer had "couple power"; they were living the life of married singles, like many people today, each involved in doing their own thing. This is a basic area where Satan aims his sharpest arrows. He loves to see us separated in our thinking and our living, a life of so-called togetherness, but separate.

Misery loves company, so Eve wanted to share her sin with her lover. "Honey, do you love me? Look what I found." Adam could have said, "You big dummy; now isn't that just like a woman? Let her out of your sight and there she is, stuffing her mouth." But he loved her, so he went into the land of death to bring her out, and he couldn't get back.

Adam's sin brought the whole race under a curse. Adam handed his God-given dominion over to another, and this evil one proceeded to rule the earth with all the disastrous effects that we see to this day. But even this miserable story has a good ending, because the last Adam came to do what the first Adam could not.

God himself came to earth as a Son, the Lord Jesus Christ. He did this to reconcile man to Himself and to put to death the deeds of the flesh (Rom. 8:13). Jesus had to go through temptation to become our High Priest. He was tempted in all points like we are (Heb. 4:15), and He used the same power that is available to us: spiritual discernment and the word of God. To every thrust of Satan, He replied with the word. "It is written, man shall not live by bread alone, but by every word that proceedeth out of the mouth of God" (Matt. 4:4). Jesus is victor, and in Him we can take our stand. In our very weakness, He is made strong!

The first thing Satan tempted Jesus with was food, and this after a forty-day fast! The first Adam fell by food and the last Adam overcame through fasting and God's word. Jesus could have turned that stone into a loaf of bread, or a roast chicken, but He refused to use any power that was not available to us, and He refused Satan's help too! He demonstrated that the spirit is stronger than the flesh.

The Old Testament is full of "object lessons" on how to meet temptation. There is a complete rundown on what happens when you resist and what happens when you don't. There is one short story in Genesis that bears repeating here because the attitude of the overcomers in this story will be helpful to us who have often stayed and looked a moment too long.

Noah, that "grand old man" who saved the human race and the animal kingdom from destruction, planted a vineyard. In due time he had some wine, and he no doubt felt as we often do—that he deserved a little treat. But he drank too much and later, in his tent, he fell asleep and kicked his covers off. Young Ham came along and saw his father drunken and naked. He stared and giggled and ran to tell his brothers. But sons Shem and Japheth took a garment and laid it on both their shoulders and *backed into the tent* to cover their father, with their faces averted so they could not look at him. That's a beautiful attitude, and one that will serve us well when Satan displays his wares.

A friend told me of once having a dream that made her wince with shame whenever she remembered it. The more she "fought" this memory, the more it came back, and always when she least wanted it. She saw that her mind had developed a pattern, a "groove." If something started to bless her, it triggered this unwanted memory. She rebuked Satan and he argued back; after all, he said, if she had never nibbled at lust, she wouldn't even know such things. . . . She asked the Lord for a solution, and He gave her the memory of the cloak of Shem and Japheth. Now when the unwanted memory came, she mentally covered it with a cloak. The memory went away and she can no longer tell you what it was. The cloak that broke the habit pattern of her mind was an attitude, repeated until it succeeded.

One day a friend and I, both on diets, were shopping together. As we strolled in an open-air mall, we passed a bakery. I was talking and soon realized that I had a one-way conversation going; I was alone. She was back at the bakery window gazing at the gooeys and moaning, "Oh, don't those look delicious!" She went off her food plan the next day; she had stayed to look a moment too long and was drawn into her own personal sin. I understood, for this had been the cause of my own downfall time and again I learned to "throw the cloak" and turn away my face.

Satan has clever tricks, but remember that he is a liar, and things never turn out the way he says they are going to. Adam and Eve found that Satan's little delights have a hook in them. They tasted good for the moment, but look what happened later! Jesus was not deceived by Satan's "reasonableness." It would be "reasonable" to eat after a long fast—but not on Satan's terms! It would be reasonable to desire lordship over His own creation, for He was the true Lord and King, but not on Satan's terms! Those temptations put before Jesus were very real, and they appealed to His deepest and perfectly legitimate desires. But they were based on disobedience, on rebellion to God, on consent to Satan the enemy.

The reason that sin is so popular and temptation is Satan's number one bestseller is this: "Sin is pleasurable." As if we didn't know! We are drawn into sin by our own lustful pleasures (James 1:13-15). It is not a sin to be tempted, but there's a difference between being tempted and entering into temptation. Sin occurs when we enter in. Thus it is important to recognize that moment when temptation is put before us and we begin to linger. . . . We couldn't help the temptation, but we can help the lingering! Scripture says that God is faithful and will not let you be tempted more than you are able to bear, and will "with the temptation also make a way to escape, that ye may be able to bear it" (I Cor. 10:13). When temptation comes upon you, look for the escape route!

C. S. Lovett's book, *Dealing with the Devil*, tells us a lot about Satan. He warns, "Have a healthy respect for your enemy and know how he operates. Have a defense system for protecting your thought life. Be equipped with the spiritual mechanics to resist Satan." We need to know something and take precautions, "lest Satan should get an advantage of us, for we are not ignorant of his devices."

Examine his devices in the context of your greatest need. Perhaps your weakest point comes at a certain time each day, or just before bedtime. Knowing this will help you set up a guard. Perhaps your weakness is for a certain food, and you can counteract this by not buying or cooking that food until you are able to overcome. If you are invited out, and you feel that you are not yet at the place where you can eat only your allowed foods while everyone gorges, make some plans for yourself. Have a "filler" food before you go, and with the edge off your appetite you will have a better chance at control. In some cases you can take along a dish for yourself made from your allowed foods. This is just common sense. In time you will be strong and the excess food won't turn you on, but at first you may need precautions, and there is nothing wrong with that. The spirit is being strengthened in the meantime according to God's plan for you.

When your warning system fails and you chance upon sin unawares, finding it lying naked before you, turn your back and cover it with your cloak! In the meantime, ask God to show you how to break the chain, the thought pattern that draws you toward your excesses. Be creative!

When you have conquered one weak spot, Satan will attack another. He can suggest, but you have a weapon. Call him by name and stick him with your sword, God's word. If you have not been used to such a personal encounter with Satan, you may feel silly "speaking" to him, but it is no laughing matter. Christ spoke to him. It is one of Satan's own devices that people don't want to recognize the reality of his existence.

Don't lose respect for Satan, but don't fear him either. Learn about him, recognize his works, and counter with your determination to be wise. He is always getting Christians to do "good" things so they won't do the best things. Don't let anything, even "good" things, keep you from feeding your spirit on God's word. It is the tool of the overcomer.

The "Lord perfects that which concerns me," and we are letting His light shine onto our eating habits right now. That's a good beginning, and it concerns us, so we can claim the Lord's perfecting strength. Who is it that nudges you to the refrigerator to eat out of time? Who is telling you that you are hungry when it is only two hours since you ate a good meal? Satan plays on the habits of the flesh like a fiddle. Then when you've eaten and start feeling guilty, who tells you that you are a rotten Christian with no testimony for the power of God? He lures and then accuses—he is no friend of yours! But his bow is broken and his tune arrested when we "keep alert and pray. Otherwise temptation will overpower you. For the spirit indeed is willing but the flesh is weak" (Matt. 25:41). Claim Rom. 8:33 and stand firmly on the sufficiency of Jesus our Lord. When Satan nudges, go to your spiritual food.

Paul knew about temptation and how to overcome: "But remember this—the wrong desires that come into your life aren't anything new and different. Many others have faced exactly the same problems before you. And, no temptation is irresistible. You can trust God to keep the temptation from becoming so strong that you can't stand up against it, for he has promised this and will do what He says. He will show you how to escape temptation's power so that you can bear up patiently against it" (I. Cor. 10:13, LB). *There's a way out and God will show it to you.* Hurrah!

One of the privileges of our inheritance is the right to use the name of Jesus. There is power in that name. You are no match for Satan, and he's not a bit afraid of you. You only make him laugh. But he is afraid of the One who overcame him, Jesus, and the use of His name puts Satan to flight. Satan knows when you merely "speak" the name like a magic incantation; but *using* it is another matter. When we *use* the name of Jesus, it means we "belong" to Him. We may not have been obeying Him perfectly, but we have been "following after." An ambassador from France can "speak" the name of England, but he cannot "use" it with authority, because he comes from another country. Christ said, "If you continue in my word, then you are truly my disciples" (John 8:31), and under those conditions we have the full privilege to use the name.

Many people call themselves Christian and even speak the name Jesus, but they have not yielded to Him, and so are without effect. Overcoming begins with yieldedness and is executed by dependence on God. For years I thought yieldedness was an emotional state and thus failed to take advantage of my privileges in Christ. The power in the name of Jesus does not come and go with your emotions. Satan has a lot of fun with this one. He makes us think we have to feel better, be more mature, somehow get ourselves "up higher" before we can call on the name of Jesus. But this is just another of his lies. Belonging to Jesus is a decision of the will; never let anyone take that truth from you.

Satan is the original "do-it-yourselfer." Every cult and false religion in the world has some kind of "do it yourself" gimmick attached to it. He tries to make us think we have to "get better" before God will have anything to do with us. But how can we get better except as God works in us? The Bible tells us that in us, that is in our flesh, dwells no good thing. So we are dependent on him from beginning to end. In salvation, we make our decision and the whole account of Jesus' righteousness is put in our name. In overcoming, we make our decision and then we start spending that account. The doing of it may not seem quite that easy, but it will be a lot easier if we understand it thoroughly right from the start.

74

Satan really gets his licks in here. He plays on all our false guilts and all our wrong programming from the world we live in to tell us that we have to get better, to earn our way, to deserve first before we can be rewarded. God's book tells us the opposite. He knows that we are beginners, and provides for that. Never let Satan rob you of your standing in Christ with his accusations. If someone is accusing you, that is Satan! God convicts, but He never accuses.

There is one other matter that needs to be dealt with on the battleground: sin. It is dealt with differently than temptation and spiritual warfare. Unconfessed sin does hinder our prayers and separates us from God. But we have clear instructions for dealing with it. Confess it and repent of it. The modern world tries to drop the word sin out of its vocabulary, but the Bible deals with it thoroughly. We need to be aware of our personal sin. Sin is very personal; what is sin to me may not be sin to you. The Greek word for sin is *hamartano* which simply means to miss the mark! We all miss the mark, sometimes with distressing frequency, but God remembered that we were "but dust," and made provision for our spiritual health. He gave us Jesus as an advocate, and He promised that if we are faithful to confess our sin, He would be faithful to forgive it and to cleanse us from all unrighteousness!

At a retreat that I attended the pastor asked, "Which is sin? Smoking, drinking, or eating too much?" A man yelled from the back, "Well, that last one sure is!" It was easy to tell which of the three did not tempt him. How we all love to condemn others and let ourselves go free! But the Holy Spirit will convict us of *our* sin, and that is all that should matter to us.

As we confess our sin to God and repent, we open the door to His healing power. As this happens we will begin to more sharply discern the temptation that has been coming to us through our own sin, and we will have more power to resist. End result: overcomers by the power of God. God doesn't care so much what we weigh, but He cares deeply about our Way. He came to show us the Life, the Truth, and the Way.

The title of the passbook to our inheritance is "watch and pray." Be honest about your weaknesses and set a watch over them. Put on God's armor. A voice within will warn when we are being enticed, and we will have penetrated Satan's disguise. When we catch him in the act and deal with him right at his work, we are getting somewhere. Speak: "Satan, in the name of Jesus, I command you to leave, for it is written, man shall not live by bread alone, but by every word that proceedeth out of the mouth of God."

To be honest with you, there were times when the food I was eating tasted so good, I didn't *want* to use the name of Jesus. Sometimes Satan came out ahead in this battle, and again, that's for your help! Don't give up just because you lose a few rounds. You see, I won a few rounds too, or Jesus won them for me, and each time I let the Lord win, I got stronger and more skillful in the use of my weapons. This is a for-real battle, and your techniques improve with usage. "Habits are made stronger every time you perform them. They are broken by not doing them."

Satan is also a flatterer: "You *deserve* better than this! You shouldn't have to suffer; you shouldn't have to deny yourself. Look at those other people, eating everything they want. . . ." No! Don't listen. He must go in Jesus' name, and he will be the loser. I failed so many times I can't count them. Yes, I gave in to the old tempter and then I would hate myself. But in the end, I was the winner and Satan the loser. I can testify that the battle became easier every time I won a victory, and you *can* get the hang of it, so stay in there!

Since we are dealing with the ground-floor problems of learning not to eat too much, I should share the very worst times I lived through. I hit a low spot soon after signing my Prayer of Agreement. After three months of cooking food I couldn't eat and washing dishes I hadn't dirtied and watching my family and friends chew and swallow food that I still loved (in fact, I still lusted for it), I found myself in tears one evening. Brooks asked me what was wrong, but I was too embarrassed to tell him.

The doorbell rang and it was a couple from our church. We visited awhile, and I could scarcely hold my tears back. I felt trapped by my diet agreement; I was hungry, and wallowing in self-pity. I invited my friend Cathy into the kitchen so we could talk, and she told me she had felt an anointing in church, so I asked her to use it to pray for me. As she prayed, I felt such a relief. God understood! He had sent someone to minister to me. Cathy turned in the Bible to Deut. 8:3 and read from the Amplified Version, "And He humbled you and allowed you to hunger, and fed you with manna . . . that He might make you recognize and personally know that man does not live by bread only, but by every word that proceeds out of the mouth of God." My eyes were opened; I had been in a test, and I had passed. I was an overcomer! God's word ministered to me more than food, and the victory tasted sweet.

Not all the battles remained that private. I'll never forget the wounds I suffered in a battle over a piece of cake. Brooks and I were attending a Marriage Encounter Seminar. It was a beautiful experience, until we got to the cake. Everyone had brought a dessert or snack food, and about thirty couples loaded the refreshment table with almost every kind of fattening food known to man. All those snack intermissions had worn down my determination. By Saturday evening, I was frantic. I decided I had to have some chocolate cake. But there was this agreement I had made with God and my husband. . . . So I asked Brooks if I could have one piece; just . . . one . . . piece. How could he refuse? He was always good to me, and he loved me and wanted me to be happy. I reminded him how good I had been for three months now, beginning with

"Honey," which usually did the trick. But he said, "No," just like that! I couldn't believe it.

That did it. Here he had been eating it up all day, and I was hungry. How unfair! I was so mad I could envision sneaking up to the auditorium and eating the whole thing. All the stubbornness and rebellion that I thought I had conquered were lying in wait for another go at me.

We had been dismissed to our rooms and told to practice our communication. It was to be the best night of the retreat, wherein we reached new levels of understanding with our mates. We closed the door on the world and were all by our intimate selves, but there was something wrong with the atmosphere. You could have cut it with a knife. When my sweetheart asked me if I wanted to practice our communication, I nearly bit his head off. "*No*, I'm not speaking to you! You won't let me have my cake!" I no longer cared how childish it sounded; I was having a temper tantrum and wasn't rational. However, I held it down because I didn't want the people in the other rooms to think that a born-again, spiritual couple like us had any problems!

Brooks just went to sleep; what else could he do? I lay in bed and God helped me to realize how childishly I had acted. That agreement had really let the pressure build so that when I blew, I couldn't ignore what I saw any more. I saw my rebellion when my "pacifier" had been snatched away. The flesh trained by the old Joan was still there. I had half planned to get up and eat some cake after Brooks went to sleep, but instead I asked God to forgive me for acting like a two-year-old. And I asked God to give me courage to ask my husband's forgiveness in the morning! God did, and I did, and Brooks did. Our weekend turned into a beautiful one, and we learned a lot about communication.

Now I've circled back to that nasty little sin, "rebellion," the root of most of our problems. Rebellion is a sin, and there is only one way to deal with sin: confess and repent. In the Old Testament they used stones! "And they shall say unto the elders of his city, this our son is stubborn and rebellious, he will not obey our voice, he is a glutton and a drunkard. And all the men of his city shall stone him with stones . . ." (Deut. 21:20, 21). Now those were strong measures, and it seems that an edict like that would straighten a person right up. But threats don't work when you are a slave to food or drink. Praise God, we have a better covenant. We have a redeemer and savior, and "by His stripes we are healed." He put us in a position to stand right before the throne of God and make our requests known, and we can ask for grace to help in time of need. The slate is cleaned in an instant when we confess our sin and repent. I will take grace instead of stones any day!

Although it doesn't recommend stones, the New Testament reiterates that food is not important. I Cor. 6:13: "For instance take the matter of eating. God has given us an appetite for food and stomachs to digest it. But that doesn't mean we should eat more than we need. Don't think of eating as important, because some day God will do away with both stomachs and food." Praise the Lord and double Hallelujah! Think of all the time wasted poring through cookbooks, shopping, cooking, and cleaning up only to start the whole cycle over every day, just to fatten up our bodies. When food is less important to us, we will have lots more time for the word of God! I found it helpful to copy verses like this and put them on the kitchen wall where I could read them often and let them permeate my thinking.

Now for some good news: there is some magic to this process after all. As we persist in feeding on good words, the higher thoughts of God, something begins to happen. Our thinking changes. Tempting displays at the store won't look so good any more. Thoughts of rich, gooey dishes will turn off more and more easily.

Years ago, I did just what my body wanted to do—sleep, eat, and lie around. And that brought me to all sorts of grief. But as you claim self-control, you will find it is a growing process (as well as a shrinking one!), and you take it one step at a time. Yesterday's mountain will become a molehill as you face today's mountain. Did you fail today? Just keep pressing toward the mark. Praise God for each new day, each new beginning, and for the victory that is already yours in Christ Jesus. Depend on Him, and He will do for you what you can't do for youself. Don't get the "I-itis" again, for it has never worked in the past and it will be your only real downfall now. Now it's Jesus the Son of God, and I can do all things through Him who strengthens me!

12 Relationship: the Answer

Our dilemma: the spirit is willing, but the flesh is weak. Mark 14:38. The answer: a relationship. Romans 7:25.

Sometimes you see ads in newspaper "personals" columns trying to locate missing heirs. An inheritance sometimes goes unclaimed because the inheritor doesn't know he has one. Don't let one of these missing heirs be you! Some Christians are so relieved at what they have been saved *from* that they fail to investigate what they have been saved *to*. But their failure in no way nullifies the truth; the inheritance is there waiting. We don't have to settle for mere "religion." The born-again Christian has something he didn't earn and doesn't deserve: sonship in the family of a King. (Someone else earned it for him.)

We are offered riches, and either we despise them or we

cannot believe they belong to us. Satan works hard to keep us deceived. Sometimes we have a false humility, a pride in being humble! But the King is not honored if we continue to act like waifs when He has made us King's sons. By a spiritual birth we were born into the family of God, and the will and testament of our Father applies to us. People should be banging on our doors asking us what it is we have that they do not have!

If you have made it this far in this book and realize that you are not a born-again believer, let me exhort you to take this step. Recognize that the world, including you, is in rebellion against its creator, God the Father, and be reconciled to the Father, by confessing your part in this rebellion and repenting of it. You might pray "Lord, have mercy on me, a sinner." Confess, repent, and accept His forgiveness. You can neither buy it nor earn it; never could you deserve it. It's a free gift by God's grace, and believing it is accepting it. There is a form of "believing" that is impersonal, with the "head" only; the Bible says that the demons believe and tremble. This is not what we mean; believing is with the heart (Rom. 10:9, 10), and culminates in love for God and men (Rom. 5:5).

Matthew tells us (15:21-28) of the Canaanite woman in the district of Tyre and Sidon who, when Jesus withdrew to her vicinity, came out and besought Him to heal her demon-possessed daughter. She used just the right words, the same words others had used when they were healed, but Jesus completely ignored her. She cried, "Have mercy on me, O Lord, Son of David," until Jesus' disciples begged Him to send her away. Whereupon he announced, "I was sent only to the lost sheep of the house of Israel." But she came and knelt before Him, "Lord, help me." And He replied, "It is not fair to take the children's bread and throw it to the dogs." How do you like that? Not exactly the sweet, compassionate Jesus we usually conjure up in our minds, is it? We'd most likely stomp angrily away if we did all that only to have Jesus call us a dog.

But what did that woman do? Get angry? Feel sorry for herself? No, she came right back without flinching, "Yes, Lord, yet even the dogs eat the crumbs that fall from their master's table." *Then* Jesus exclaimed, "O woman, great is your faith! Be it done for you as you desire." Her daughter was healed instantly.

Results count and that woman got results. We search for the secret formula from others who've gotten results. We ask, what church did you go to? What book did you read? What words did you say in your prayer? So, we attend that church, read that book, and say that prayer—and we get *the silent treatment* from Jesus. Why? Because we don't want to go through what the Canaanite woman went through. She endured the humiliation of being unmasked for what she was. She had prayed as though she were a Jew with a claim on the lineage of David. *She was pretending to be something she wasn't.* Judson Cornwall says, "The only way to get what you want is to admit what you are." So she knelt before Him and acknowledged the truth about herself. We need to do the same when we find our formulas don't work.

If God tells you you're a glutton, admit it and fall at His feet for healing mercy. Don't run away or fool yourself by deciding, "I'll never eat too much again." Both of those responses are just our flesh still trying to do it without Jesus. God speaks to us in many ways: through the Bible, circumstances, other people, and, directly, through the ears of our hearts. Learn to listen— the way of a fool is right in his own eyes, but a wise man listens to advice—and ask God to confirm the truth. The truth hurts, but it won't kill you, it will set you free. So let's confess our sins and get the cleansing and change of heart that only God can give.

I'm not talking here about an initial conversion experience, either. We should continue to walk in Christ as we first received Him, as sinners in need of grace. The reason we don't want to do this is not because it will bring disgrace on the gospel or minimize what Jesus has done for us; those are only pious-sounding ruses. The truth is, as one woman put it, "we're too proud to be honest."

You don't need to confess your sins to the whole church. Sometimes it's appropriate in a small group, sometimes with a private confessor, and sometimes all alone with God. But we must remember that no person or group, only Jesus, can save us. "Are you so foolish and so senseless and so silly? Having begun [your new life spiritually] with the (Holy) Spirit, are you now reaching perfection [by dependence] on the flesh?" (Galatians 3:3, Ampl. version).

Formulas are great for mathematical calculations, scientific problems, and chemical cleaners, but we can never substitute them for our relationship with God, wherein God is free to act unexpectedly. Once we experience a breakthrough of faith—like the Canaanite woman—the Lord may give us a formula of our own. It is guaranteed to work; it will carry us past the silence of God because it is established in faith in the character of the God of the Bible, not in the formula. That breakthrough of faith comes when we embrace the humiliation of total honesty about ourselves. The end of such a breakthrough is invariably total victory.

That is good news for the overweight. We won't have to "diet" for the rest of our lives; we can change our way of life. Further, we will *like* it this way! We will be able to eat what we want because we will *want* what is right for us. Yes, you will have to set up a watchman for a while: "Put a watch, O Lord, before my mouth" (Psa. 141:3). When the flesh no longer craves the old ways, you will be free indeed! The book adds further promises to those who love Him: "God will make all things work together for good" (Rom. 8:28), and "in all things we will overwhelmingly conquer through Him who loved us" (v. 37). *Listen!* That is saying that one day we will even praise

God that we were fat, because it was turned in for good by bringing us to the path of the overcomer!

Clinton White, the alcoholic who was a "hopeless case" for fourteen years, found this way out. He had been dried out, wrung out, psyched out, scolded, nursed, cursed; you name it, he'd had it. He had even failed in AA! Nothing worked. *Then* he found the new birth and became a new creature in Christ Jesus. He says, "I didn't just change my ways; I am a different man, a new man. Who is that lazy, wicked wretch in my past? He is another man. I have a new identity, new values, and a new hope! Because of this I am a new man. When the other man faced a crisis, he ran at once to the bottle and drank himself out of reality. The new man never even thinks of running from the reality of difficulties by drinking them away. The old man suffered every day from worry; the new man has faced intense pressure with peace of heart. . . . If you think I am an ex-drunk telling how he reformed, you will never know what really happened to me. I did not reform. *I am a new man.* The old Clinton White was an alcoholic. When he wanted to stay sober he waged a daily battle, and he invariably lost. The new Clinton White doesn't even have to fight this battle because he is not an alcoholic. Alcohol is no longer considered as a way out . . . !"

Christian, born of the spirit, new creature in Christ Jesus, you are not going to be a "sober foodaholic." That is why the very best diets often fail; they are done in the power of the flesh and the graduate is a sober foodaholic. He must maintain a battle for life. But, by the power of God, you can change to a new life style and your flesh will no longer want the excesses it once fed upon. You've just heard some good news!

We know we cannot depend on the flesh, for it is self-serving and brings you back to itself. It proves unworthy every time (Rom. 8:26). But we have made a covenant with One who can be depended and relied on to deliver us from the power of the flesh. The "prayer of agreement and controlled eating" was our covenant, and we can depend on God to go more than halfway in this covenant. We could not keep the law, so He gave us grace. We could not be righteous, so He was righteous for us, and imputed His own righteousness to our account. We could not keep our word, so He gave us His. We were weak and He imparted strength. We were orphaned, and He restored us to His family. We have something that we can depend on!

The only stipulation is that you *accept* what is offered. God's offering came with a name: Jesus. God's covenant gives us everything we cannot obtain for ourselves: salvation, abundant life, eternal life. Love. Joy. Peace. Satisfaction. "Abundance," says Mr. Webster, is "overflowing fulness, ample sufficiency, great plenty." It is probably more than that, for words fail us. Only the Holy Spirit who praises in sounds that cannot be uttered can probe God's abundance.

How can we, how dare we, be lazy and dull of hearing when so much is offered to us? We have found the secret to overcoming: victory lies through growth in the spirit of, and complete dependence on, Jesus the victor. This is our bank account and He has written our passbook. You, dear weak one, will have cause to shout louder than anyone, because in overcoming your weakness, you will learn something that others of God's children have not learned: moment-by-moment relationship with the Strong One, Jesus the Lord. This relationship will develop a trust pattern that will move mountains, not just the mountain of fat!

Relationship involves prayer, praise, commitment, agreement, worship, self-honesty, listening, and *hearing*. Then, as we read His word, we are listening to our Father. It will not be legalistic and negative, but alive with the Spirit. Read the will and testament of all you have inherited and learn of your family rights and privileges. Then you will no longer be a "missing heir."

13 Believing Is Good, but Relying Is Better

Most blessed is the man who believes in, trusts in, and relies on the Lord, and whose hope and confidence the Lord is. Jeremiah 17:7 Ampl.

My pastor, Merlin Carothers, tells how his platoon acted during World War II when they heard a certain word. Before hearing the word, they were busy preparing for battle. They had cleaned their rifles, filled their bandoleers with ammunition, and dug their foxholes. Then the word came: **"Victory."**

They threw down their rifles and leaped out of their foxholes. They danced, hollered, laughed, and threw their helmets on the ground. Their circumstances had not changed all that much. They were still a long way from home, they were still in the army, and their food still consisted of field rations. The only thing that had changed was that an announcement had been made. And they chose to believe it! They went even further: *they relied on it.*

They could have said, "Maybe it isn't so," and stayed in their foxholes with their rifles ready, their feet in the mud and their eyes toward the enemy. Or they could have believed, but stayed in the foxholes to be safe. Sounds silly, but that is just what many Christians are doing today: still on the defensive even though victory has been announced.

A word of authority has been passed on to us that has the power of completed victory behind it. We place ourselves on the winning side when we believe it. That platoon of weary soldiers believed the word because of who said it; their own field commander had passed the word to them. We can believe in the victory because of who won it. Almighty God, in the person of the Son Jesus Christ, came to earth, took on a body of flesh, and won the victory. Believing it puts you in possession of that account where His own righteousness is imputed to you. The account is yours and no one can take it away; that's the message of the gospel. What remains is to put this account to use, to bring its power into your daily life. You do this when you learn to *rely* on it; there's a difference between believing it's there and relying on it.

You've probably heard the story of a man who planned to take a wheelbarrow across a rope strung over Niagara Falls. He asked several people if they believed he could do it, and they had heard of his reputation, so they all assured him they believed it. Then he said, "OK, if you believe it, get in the wheelbarrow and go with me." Nobody went. And that's how Christians often act. We believe the Lord can do what he says, but we aren't willing to get in the wheelbarrow.

We already have the promise that believing will take us from death to life. We have a new position, a whole new "frame of reference." Whereas we were poor, now we are rich; we have a spiritual inheritance. But too often the Christian only assents to this truth, and fails to put it to the test by relying on it. An overcomer is one who has learned to rely in this inheritance; he makes withdrawals from the account and uses it!

There is a way to gain the courage to get in the wheelbarrow. Study the person who is running it. Is he trustworthy? The book tells us that He is creator of the universe, and by Him all things consist. He doesn't need a spaceship to get to Mars because He is the one who put Mars in its place a long time ago. After telling us of the unfathomable greatness of our God, the book plugs all that power into YOU by telling you that this same creator loved you from all eternity. He knows you by name and its not just a passing acquaintance; He knows how many hairs there are on your head. He not only drives the barrow, but controls the rope and the river as well. And further, He is more interested in *you* than in all the rest of creation because you were created in His own image. The book is threaded through with assurances of God's supreme interest in *you*. It will be easy to start relying on Him when you spend time in the book, the manual that tells us how to make the unseen, eternal verities "work."

We don't have any trouble trusting in and even relying on the things we see. I trusted in a camp cot one time and it let me down. Not only that, it advertised my problem to several witnesses and gave them all a good laugh. Brooks and I went on an outing with another couple and some borrowed camping equipment. The only slim person among us was Brooks. We tried to be extra careful of the equipment, since it didn't belong to us; but it was getting old, and it was downright diabolical how one piece after another gave way. Our friends each broke a chair, and even Brooks put his foot through something. I was the only one who hadn't broken anything and along about midnight, I was feeling smug about it. All was quiet in the camp and I began to giggle. When you weigh 230 pounds, you are grateful for a chance to laugh at somebody else! But I got

89

carried away with it, and laughed too hard. Right at midnight in Yosemite National Forest, my cot gave way and left me hugging the ground.

If I was willing to rely on a rotten camp cot, why couldn't I rely on the unseen but much more dependable reality of Christ? (II Cor. 4:18). All the other visible objects that we rely on are doomed to the same fate as the camp cot no matter how sturdy they might appear. Sooner or later they decay or rust and go back to the elements. The contrast between seen and unseen even shows up in a way in the birth, life, and death of a tree. Unseen nutrients and elements emerge as fiber, leaves and fluids that we can see. But the moment that tree is born, or becomes "seen," it is subject to death. The chair you are relying on will some day be a rotten heap, but when it rots, it will return to the elements and re-enter the unseen state. Then it will again be available to the process that makes and sustains visible life. In this limited sense it is "eternal" and illustrates the difference between visible transience and invisible permanence.

So our trust ought to be put in the unseen eternal since what is seen is temporary, like that cot. Our unseen, living God is the trustworthy author of life that is real and permanent. And the overcoming Christian knows that He alone can produce tangible results that last when we learn to rely on Him!

We fatties have not trusted much except our daily intake of food, which definitely turns into the "seen." But the trustworthy power that we can depend on is that the spirit will grow stronger in us so that it will have control of the body. Our priority, then, is to feed the spirit more faithfully than we feed the body, so it will grow to be the stronger of the two. We can depend on the results, because God has spoken it. The announcement has been made. Paul's message is this plain: If we are willing to trust the objects around us, knowing their end, how much more should we trust the living God who is eternal.

Another problem for fatties is that we are "failure oriented." People are made of the same defective clay as ourselves, and they tend to disappoint us. But it is an insult to attribute these human failings to Jesus, the author and finisher of our faith. He did not fail. He proved His sufficiency to the death and beyond—to the resurrection from the dead! Our failures and disappointments in the past need not hinder us. We have a Lord who is victor. He proved that the unseen force is stronger than life itself, and by a process that is also unseen but just as sure, His victory becomes our victory.

Overcoming is a principle, and it works. Give it the right input, and the outcome is assured. If an enemy has robbed you of your birthright, self-control, you will defeat him when you eat of the word of God which nourishes victory. It is a sure thing, because God made us in His own image, and when we take in the words of God there is that within us which responds. If you weigh 500 pounds, or even more, you can begin to act victorious! Jump up and down and shout *victory*. Rejoice, yell, and throw your bayonet away (the one you kept sticking yourself with).

Christ said that He put all things under His feet, and that includes the refrigerator and the kitchen stove. "All things" means everything that has ever defeated you plus anything Satan can suggest that you may not know about yet. That's the good word, and it should cause us to leap out of our foxholes and throw our helmets on the ground!

14 Bread Alone

Feed me with the food that is needful for me. Proverbs 30:8, Ampl.

"What can I eat?"

There was a time when I would have turned to this chapter first, and perhaps that is what you have done. I was hoping to see in print that I could eat anything I wanted and still lose weight. Now, there is a sense in which this will become true, because your *wanter* can change by God's power. But change takes time, and during that time you will need to exercise skill in recognizing and breaking the old habits.

The victory road begins with a decision, which you have made. It requires discernment and self-honesty in recognizing the roots of the problem so you can begin the healing process in the right place. For this we have the "ever-present help" of the

Word and Spirit of our God. And it requires some practical steps at the root level! Our real problem began in our minds years ago, probably in early childhood. And working out from this point, we have learned to plan, shop, and cook in ways that cater to our weakness. We have acquired habits of hoarding, snacking, licking, sneaking, what have you.

This chapter deals with some practical steps to change these ways, and some plain facts about food. Some foods just cannot be eaten if you are going to lose weight. Cakes and milkshakes won't lose their calories because you pray over them! In addition to being loaded with calories, these sweet gooeys are "deceitful foods" because they cause addiction to themselves. We can be delivered of this addiction, but not while we are eating them!

Prominent among the addictive foods are sugar, coffee, and chocolate. Notice that your cravings are most often for sugar foods, salty foods, or starchy foods. Your body can build a dependency on these foods just as it would for alcohol, cigarettes, drugs. Certain foods, especially sugar foods, are like alcohol to the alcoholic. To susceptible people, a craving is set up that is just as demanding as alcohol or drugs. The good news is that this craving will go away when it is starved out.

Some diets tell you to eat everything, just "small portions." I believe the reason such diets have so little success with people addicted to certain foods is because they continue to feed the craving, and as soon as the period of self-discipline is over, the old craving takes charge. On these diets, you have to count calories carefully, exercise supreme self-control, and starve in the midst of plenty. Overweight people are short on self-control to begin with, and they have a weakness which will not go away if it is fed daily. Determining those weaknesses and refusing to feed them for as long as it takes to break their "grip" on you is plain common sense. The appetite can be re-trained to *like* the proper and needful foods.

It has been my experience that when I eliminated sugar foods, for which I had a great weakness, I gradually lost the craving for them. Nutritionists tell us that the chemistry of the body in some people sets up a type of "body alcohol" from certain addictive foods that gains control just as alcohol gains control of the alcoholic.

At the other extreme from the "small portions" diet is the unbalanced, monotony diet. I am not going to recommend such an unhealthful diet. I do recommend that people with a real weakness for sugar and/or certain carbohydrates guard their exposure to them until they lose the undue craving for them. Substitute healthful, nourishing foods that are also palatable. In most instances, the dieter will eat healthier meals than ever before.

My definition of a crash diet is one you fall off of, usually face first into a lot of fattening food. You may lose weight on a freaky diet, but you don't learn how to eat. Your appetite is merely held in abeyance, and when it lets go, look out! Most overeaters have gained and lost a thousand pounds. My clothes used to be the expando model; they could get bigger or smaller as needed. Now I can buy the overcomer's model because my appetite has been re-trained.

Changing a life style takes longer than "dieting," but it has the advantage of being permanent. For once in our lives we need to nip the urge to hurry. Remember the tortoise and the hare. In the past we were always like the hare; once we made up our minds to diet, we were in a big hurry to get it over with so we could eat again. We plunged in like crazy, then we began to dither and loiter, and finally fell asleep at the job. When we woke up, it was to the discouraging realization that we were still fat! The tortoise only plodded, but he got there first in spite of that. We already know that spectacular "on again off again" diets don't work, so let's ask God for patience and determination this time to change our life style. "Run the race with patience" (Heb. 12:1); "faith and patience inherit the promises" (Heb. 6:12); "for ye have need of patience" (Heb. 10:36).

In our new life style there is latitude in choosing a food plan. It is important to choose a plan that fits you, one that you can be happy and comfortable with. You need an eating plan that you can stay with for the rest of your life, not something of someone else's choosing that helps you lose but sooner or later drives you berserk so that you gain it all back. There will be restrictions during the weight loss period that may not be necessary later on, but basically the plan is to make a real change in habits, in desires, and purpose for your life.

If you are overweight, there are few things you could do that would be more worthwhile for you than taking some time *now* to develop a food plan that you can stay on. A standard excuse today is that you are "too busy." But a life style that glorifies God the creator, should not be one of the things you are "too busy" for.

Our principle aim is a new life style in which food loses its overimportance to us. We need to ask God for a new attitude toward food. We need to ask Him to change us so we *like* an eating plan that is satisfying and natural, yielding health, energy, and joy. During the weight loss period itself, we will have to pay some attention to what we eat and don't eat, but the goal is to be set free from the dominion of food in our lives.

It may help you to think of your weight-loss period as a "partial fast." In the Old Testament we read of partial fasts which allowed some foods but "no pleasant thing." Our diet will be pleasant enough, but it will eliminate some of the foods we have considered pleasant in the past. If you dedicate this as a fast unto the Lord, it will help you stay on your plan and give you a spiritual blessing. When Corrie and Betsie ten Boom were on starvation rations in the German prison camp, Betsie suggested that they dedicate this involuntary fast to the Lord so they could at least reap a spiritual blessing from it. They did and it did; Corrie noticed that from that day they had greater victory over the evil forces around them.

Is there a certain food you love more than all the rest? How do you feel when it's on the table and someone else gets the last piece or serving of it? Are you still a joyful person when you can't have it? Do you ever feel hungry in such a way that nothing, apart from that one thing, will satisfy you? How do you feel when you've just sat down to enjoy this food and you're interrupted by the phone or doorbell? How would you feel if a member of your family told you to quit eating that food, or even took it away from you?

Your answers to these questions should show you a lot about the true nature of your attachment to your favorite food. How does it compare with your attachment to Jesus? Is there a conflict between them? Have you ever considered giving that favorite food as a love offering to Jesus? He gave himself up to torture and death because He loves us.

A love offering is taking the food you love the most and offering it up to Jesus because you love Him more. Ken Copeland tells about his own experience with this that, every time he is faced with the temptation to eat this food, he begins to repeat over and over, "I choose Jesus, I choose Jesus."

God will honor our decision to "sacrifice" our favorite food. Will you decide today? I was tired of carrying my idols—I had several of them, including some health food desserts—around with me. Finally, one day, I decided to give them to God. Choose today what your love sacrifice will be.

Another plain fact that has to be faced is that the new life style will take more planning and perhaps more cooking time than the old style. (But it also promises renewed energy that more than makes up the difference.) Lazy snacks must go; vegetable and protein dishes take their place. We will recommend some of these foods in plentiful amounts, some to be eaten with temperance. A few foods are to be treated like alcohol—pray for deliverance from the craving!

It may seem like a contradiction to say that we want to be delivered from thinking about food all day and then say that we will have to spend more time "planning" our new life style. That is because we already have certain habits which are so ingrained that we don't really think about them; we just do them. To change that style takes some thought, determination, and action. When our new style has become a habit, we will be "set free." Although we might spend more time cooking meats and a variety of vegetables than we did "jamming together" gooey casseroles, we won't be spending as much of our time thinking about what we are going to eat and then regretting having eaten it.

There was a time when people had to hunt their food, kill and dress it, plant and reap and thresh it, then grind it and cook it by slow processes. The process itself caused them to put in more hours working for it than they did eating it. Compare that time to this one. We drive to the supermarket and fill our baskets with prepared, ready-to-eat, fattening foods, drive home and start eating. I usually ate some on the way home. Some foods take a little defrosting, but there is plenty to eat while we wait. Such an eating pattern doesn't seem like an "obvious sin" at the time, but it gets obvious soon enough.

For good health we need "living foods." A good criterion for your new shopping list is to make it mostly the foods that grow. These foods satisfy and nourish, and most of them have fiber content, which is more important than most of us realize. One medical report that I read said that cancer of the colon was much more prevalent in people on a low-fiber diet. As basic needs are satisfied, the body will stop craving foods it has been addicted to.

Developing a plan that fits you is good judgment and common sense. You will need to juggle what appeals to you, what fits your needs, what you can afford, and what satisfies without fattening. Be honest in assessing your weaknesses, and plan to avoid them at first. Later, when you are stronger, the ready-made tempters will no longer look so good. Every time you go forth and conquer, it will get easier. The effort you spend on planning, shopping and cooking according to your new life style is more than half the battle. The eating problem is more than half-solved by the time you get to the table.

In the meantime, your attitudes will gradually change as your mind is exposed to the good words of God. As you set your will, renew your mind, and practice your new style with God's help, the flesh will begin to follow along like an automaton. It has, after all, been designed to follow where it is led. It is not some monster that lives a life of its own, although it may have seemed that way in the past. It is subject to the control of the mind! Learning to wage the battle of the mind has been the subject of this book.

Don't expect too much of yourself. This too is a downfall. Have patience with yourself! Don't let Satan accuse you, which he will. Tell him to begone and start again. The important thing is that now you have a plan; before you had none. Your plan may need to be revised and perfected as you go along, but you have a start. You are no longer "empty-headed." One of the things that disquiets the earth (see Prov. 30:21-22 Ampl.) is an "empty headed fool when he is filled with food." So cheer up; the head is no longer empty, but filled with a good plan that is augmented daily by the higher thoughts of God. This combination *will* win, so don't let anyone cause you to give it up!

After you have chosen your plan, the place to begin is when you write your shopping list. It is important to write out your list, especially at first, or your old habit pattern will go into gear at the grocery store and you will come out with the same old stuff. Two important pointers: Don't go shopping when you are hungry. It's much easier to carry out a plan for future eating right after you have eaten. Also, go to the departments where the "living foods" are and put them in your basket first. Then most of your money will already be committed and you will be less tempted by the old fatteners. I used to fill my basket with all the foods I craved, then had to economize on meats and vegetables!

The natural, living foods are fresh vegetables, fruits, grains, meats, and dairy products. The "dead foods" are the highly refined foods. They are expensive and in many instances they do little to nourish. Many overeaters are tired, run down, and even sick because a large part of their diets are made of "dead" foods.

To be a foodaholic, compulsive eater or glutton, food must first of all taste good. It should be fattening and loaded with either sugar, flour or salt. If it does not fit into any of these categories, then it is not food, it is medicine.

A glutton's glossary of foods would go something like this:

Pie	good food
Ice Cream	excellent food
Cake	great finger food (when no one's looking)
Cookies	good—they travel well and can be swallowed whole in emergencies
Spaghetti	tremendous—the more the better
Bread	the staff of life—"stuff of life"—six slices average serving
Noodles	a real delicacy—tiny morsels
Peanuts	wonderful for elephants and over-eaters

Peanut Butter	it really sticks with you—in more ways than one
Soda Pop	a real thirst quencher
Zucchini	medicine—to be eaten only when forced or starving
Egg Plant	medicine—unless covered with Italian sauce to cover up the taste
Spinach	to be eaten by children and Popeye
Fruit	food—especially good when in pie; a lot of it is best

But food is actually fuel. Webster's defines food as "nutritive material taken into an organism for growth, work or repair and for maintaining the vital process." Food falls into three main categories: carbohydrates, fats and proteins.

Let's define good foods and junk foods (the Bible calls them deceitful foods or "dainties"). Good food is what God made, and junk food is what man made. (There are exceptions for those desiring to lose weight, and we'll cover this later.)

This brings us to the three guidelines for healthy eating:

1. Eat only the foods that spoil and eat them before they do.
2. When shopping for groceries, only buy the foods that you think Jesus, Peter or Paul would buy.
3. If God made it and man didn't change it, then you can eat it (see later explanation).

Carbohydrates

"Bread is a carbohydrate and it will cause you to gain weight," says one doctor, while another doctor tells us, "You can't get fat on bread, it's a complex carbohydrate."

Who is right? Let's define some terms. In Webster's dictionary, carbohydrate is defined as any group of neutral compounds, composed of carbon, hydrogen and oxygen, including the sugars and starches, etc. Carbohydrate foods are either natural or refined (processed). The following lists are not complete, but are meant to help you see the difference.

1. *Natural Carbohydrates*

apples	oranges
corn	carrots
wheat	potatoes
beans	grains
honey	rye
nuts	peas
milk	brown rice
juices	

2. *Processed Carbohydrates*

cakes	jams, jellies
cookies	chips
pretzels	ice cream
white rice	puddings
boxed cereals	pies
crackers	pasta
noodles	sugar
alcohol	

Natural carbohydrates are important to good health. But, our body will turn protein into carbohydrates. It won't turn carbohydrates into protein.

Sugar Content in Fruits and Vegetables

It's possible to consume two full cups of sugar daily, without ever having one crystal of refined sugar (sucrose, brown, white, raw, molasses, etc.). Honey, sorghum, maple sugar, etc. are a high source, but grains also have a high sugar (carbohydrate) percentage. There follows a table of sugar content in fruits and vegetables. As you work to maintain your weight, you don't want to gain back ugly pounds by eating the wrong kind of fruits and vegetables. This especially applies to those who are carbohydrate sensitive!

Sugar Percentage Charts

For weight loss, limit your fruits to below 10% and occasionally a 15% serving daily.

Fresh Fruits:

7%	10%	15%	20%	30%	Over 30%
Loganberries	Pineapples	Huckleberries	Bananas	Persimmons	Apricots
Avocadoes	Blackberries	Apples	Plums		(dried)
Grapefruits	Cantaloupes	Apricots	Figs		Apples
Lemons	Cranberries	Cherries			(dried)
Strawberries	Muskemelons	Currants			Prunes
Olives	Oranges	Grapes			Raisins
Watermelons	Peaches	Nectarines			
	Raspberries	Orange Juice			
		Pears			

Keep serving sizes the same. One cup for vegetables under 10%, and one-half cup for 10% to 15%. (See next page.)

Your body uses carbohydrates as a source of energy, but it always stores any surplus in the form of fat for future use. The amount of carbohydrate that can be converted into fat is limit-

Vegetables:

3%	5%	10%	15%	20%
Asparagus	Beets	Carrots	Lima Beans	Corn
Brussels Sprouts	Cabbage	Celery Root	(canned)	(fresh)
Celery	Cauliflower	Onions-green	Peas-green	Lima Beans
Cucumbers	Onions-dry	Parsnips	(fresh)	(fresh)
Eggplant	Peppers-green	Peas (canned)	Sweet Potatoes	
Kale	Pumpkin	Rutabagas	Yams	
Leeks	Radishes	Squash-hubbard	Brown Rice	
Lettuce	Green Beans	Turnips	(cooked)	
Rhubarb	Watercress			
Spinach				
Squash-cream				
Squash-Italian				

less. To a person who is overweight and doesn't have a sensitive pancreas, just cutting out man-made carbohydrates is sufficient.

When we eat carbohydrates, our bodies readily convert them into sugar which is sent straight into our blood streams. Almost invariably we get more sugar than we need for energy and the pancreas responds by sending insulin into the blood stream to convert that excess sugar to fat for storage. The pancreases of fatties, who characteristically gorge themselves on carbohydrates, become overactive trying to contain the floods of sugar that are arriving almost incessantly from the stomach. As a result they commonly over-kill the sugar, which produces, in turn, a run-down, listless feeling and intense hunger which sends the glutton back for more food sooner.

Fats

Fat is defined as "any animal tissues consisting chiefly of cells distended with greasy or oily matter; adipose tissue; also this oily or greasy substance or like substance in plants, in certain seeds; also such substance used in cookery, or any class of compounds of carbon, hydrogen and oxygen (of which the natural fats are mixtures)."

Fats, just like carbohydrates, can be used in only two ways. To meet current energy needs or be stored as fat for future energy uses. Neither fats nor carbohydrates can be used to build muscle tissue, blood or bone. Even though both fats and carbohydrates are used for energy there is a great difference in the way the body uses them.

When more carbohydrates are absorbed into your body than can be used immediately for energy, it must be changed into body fat at once or be lost in the bloodstream (as with diabetics). Excess fat is not immediately changed into permanent body fat, it is held in a temporary storage in the liver and the lymphatic vessels until it is needed at a later time in the body for energy and then it is dispatched when needed.

Fat alone will not make you fat! The eskimos lived for years on fat and they survived quite well, but, personally, whale blubber never did much for me. It is when we eat fats and carbohydrates together that we get fat! Bread and butter, potato with butter or sour cream, granola and all baked products made with oil, butter, etc.

Fat is not as bad as it looks (it never looked good on me, though). Fats in diet do serve an important purpose. Fat promotes normal growth, keeps the skin soft and supple, and influences the rate at which your bones calcify. The gall bladder also needs oil to function properly.

Without fats in the diet, certain vitamins couldn't enter your digestive tract. Vitamins A, D and E are fat soluble. Fat is the vehicle these vitamins need to enter the bloodstream and lymphatic vessels. Even if you took these vitamins in capsule form, they still couldn't be absorbed without fats in the diet.

It has been medically proved that refined carbohydrates can be eliminated from your diet with no ill effects whatever; but that neither proteins nor fat can be eliminated from the diet, if you are to remain in good health. All reducing diets work on the principle of either low calories, low fat or low carbohydrate. The amount of fats allowed depends on which eating plan you choose to live with, but never, never go without at least one or two tablespoons of oil daily.

What is the best kind of fat to eat? Dr. Keith Lowell told the delegates of a recent convention, "Liquid oils such as safflower, sesame, etc. are best. Corn oil is not as good. Margarine isn't good because they use a chemical to hydrogenate it and make it hard."

Protein

What is a protein? Protein is the number one diet item for healthy living. If proteins don't come first in our diets, we shortchange ourselves. Proteins are made up of carbon, hydrogen, oxygen and nitrogen. Some contain sulfur and a few have iodine in them.

Dr. Lawson, a noted nutritionist, says there are thirty-two amino acids. Only twenty-two of them are understood. Nutritionists tell us that if we get eight of these in our food we can manufacture all the others in our digestive canal. The eight essential amino acids are isoleucine, leucine, lysine, methionine, phenylalanine, tryptophane, threonine and valine.

If a protein contains these essentials, it's called a complete protein. (Some authorities say we also need arginine and histidine for quick growth and emergency healing.) Every part of our body relies on protein for proper growth. Cathryn Elwood says that "The foundation ingredient, protoplasm, which is the living jellylike substance of every cell, is protein. No protein, no protoplasm, no life" (*Feel Like a Million*, p. 9).

I am not a vegetarian (although my daughter, Christa, is). But it is my opinion that it is a healthy way to live. I made that statement in one of our monthly magazines and received more mail than I had in months, and the ones who wrote in were angry. The Bible is very plain when it says that "one man's faith permits him to believe he may eat anything [referring to meat], while a weaker one [limits his] eating to vegetables. Let not him who eats look down on or despise him who abstains and let not him who abstains criticize and pass judgment on him who eats; for God has accepted and welcomed him" (Romans 14:2, 3). Far too many Americans gorge on meat and starve of other sources of protein. Temperance is the key.

I would enjoy being a vegetarian except for one reason: I gain weight when I eat that way. Many doctors, nutritionists and vegetarians will argue about this, but the fact of personal experience remains, not only for me, but for hundreds of other former foodaholics.

Let's cover the merits of vegetable protein first, then animal protein, so that we can decide which to choose for weight loss. As you can see, this is where the difference between cooking for health and for losing weight comes in. I didn't understand this, until we asked Dr. Bill Yarwood to speak at a retreat. At the time, I ate things that prevented further weight loss and I was completely ignorant as to why. All the foods I ate were for optimum health, but I wasn't losing any more weight.

In ancient times, men often ate more vegetable than animal protein, because animal protein was more difficult to obtain (first you had to catch it and then the work began). It was eaten mostly on special occasions. Vegetable protein is stored more easily and keeps for longer periods of time. To store animal protein requires some method of preservation (canning, freezing, refrigeration, etc.).

I used to think—because I had been told so—that animal proteins are superior to vegetable proteins. But one of the world's leading centers for nutritional research, the Max Planck Institute in Germany, has discovered that many vegetables, fruits, seeds nuts and grains are excellent sources of protein (Paavo Airola, *Are You Confused?*, p. 24). Recent research reveals two important facts before unknown to science:

1. Vegetable proteins are higher in biological value than animal proteins.
2. Raw proteins have higher biological value than cooked proteins. You need only one-half the amount of protein if you eat raw vegetable proteins instead of cooked animal proteins. (Airola, p. 32.)

Let me repeat that I am not a vegetarian at this time, nor am I a Seventh Day Adventist, but facts are facts. The question is, are meat eaters healthier than vegetarians, as is supposed?

The Seventh Day Adventists who don't eat meat for religious reasons have forty percent fewer coronary diseases, four hundred percent fewer deaths from respiratory diseases, a thousand percent lower death rate from lung cancer, and fifty percent fewer dental caries among their children. This study was made by reputable medical men and reported in the *Journal of the American Medical Association* according to Paavo Airola (*Are You Confused?*, pp. 34-35). I'm sure that there are factors, beside their abstinence from meat, which contribute to this remarkable health record. They also don't smoke or drink. And the ones I've known teach the importance of having a born-again experience with Christ as savior.

The precedents for a life style that involves the eating of vegetable protein more often and in greater quantities than animal protein are ancient and widespread. And it's undeniably the healthiest way to live. But it is frequently difficult to lose weight while eating this way. Why? The answer to that lies in what eating refined carbohydrates from childhood up does for your body.

Less affluent peoples, like the Bulgarians, and remote tribesmen, like the Mayas of the Yucatan Peninsula, grow up eating natural foods with an emphasis on complex carbohydrates and vegetable protein. But we Americans grow up on daily servings of doughnuts, french fries, and pastries. The damage such a diet does to a growing body is serious and, usually, longstanding. Consuming sugar and junk food produces an abnormal carbohydrate metabolism. What this means is that our bodies have become so adept at handling the junk-food carbohydrates that our pancreases are working overtime to produce the insulin to change the sugar into fat. Thus, no matter how high quality, complex, raw, or natural the carbohydrate is that we eat, it tends to be quickly and indiscriminatly converted to fat by our peculiarly-trained bodies.

Protein cannot be quickly converted to sugar, and thus to fat, and animal protein is relatively unaccompanied by carbohydrate when compared with vegetable protein (that is, a steak contains much less carbohydrate than a serving of beans and rice, although both are substantial sources of complete protein). For this reason I recommend that you use animal protein (meat, eggs, etc.) in your weight-loss eating plan. *But only in limited quantities.* Those diets that encourage your gluttony by telling you to eat all the meat and fat you want are wrong. They serve only to indulge the self-life, whereas our aim is to bring every thought captive to obey Christ. We need God to change our hearts so that we'll produce the fruit of the Spirit, which includes self-control.

God will heal you so that, by prayer and discipline, your abnormal metabolism can become normal, your pancreas desensitized. When, in time, that has happened to you, you can begin to eat a more normal diet which will include wholesome, natural foods that are nevertheless high in carbohydrate or fat content, like fresh fruit and milk. In the meantime, don't feel sorry for yourself—after all, whom can we blame? We're the ones who used to brag, "I can't believe I ate the whole thing!"

And if you're lamenting the reduction of meat in your diet, think about this. America pays a price for its luxurious diet that derives its protein almost solelty from animal sources. We are far ahead of most of the rest of the world when it comes to cancer, heart disease, arthritis, obesity, high blood pressure, multiple sclerosis, miscarriages, birth deformities, and several other degenerative diseases. We've prayed that God would heal our land, now let's do works meet for repentance by choosing the food that will help our bodies rather than hinder them. After all, our bodies are the temples of the Holy Spirit; it's time we stopped treating them like garbage cans.

Natural foods to avoid if you want to lose weight

Please note, these foods are excellent for good nutrition and should be included in the diet, unless through years of wrong eating you have a damaged metabolism. Begin to use these foods in small amounts after you've allotted time for your metabolism to be healed:

Peas, beans (except green and wax), lentils, nuts, milk, yogurt, cereals, cowpeas, soybeans, peanuts, nut preparations, wheat, malt, honey, some fruits (see chart on page 103), starchy vegetables such as potatoes and cereals, and all dried fruits. This is not a complete list, but it will give you an idea as to what can be very beneficial to the health of many people and still hinder weight loss.

Questions:
1. **Why don't you suggest yogurt for weight loss?** It's true that many civilizations have thrived on yogurt, but it is not the

type bought in the market today with added sugar, fruit and who knows what else. It is the sour fermented yogurt (plain, unflavored) that no overeater considers to be food. Yogurt is very easily digested, high in carbohydrates and a tremendous health plus for normal people. If the "loser" eats yogurt, it should be the unflavored variety and in small amounts (that's no problem if it's sour, right?).

2.   **I thought honey was much better than sugar, so why can't I eat it and still lose weight?** Because it's higher in calories and carbohydrates than sugar, although it is a real food and not addictive like sugar. By all means, switch to honey for cooking and baking at home; but it is tremendously fattening. Please remember that this section is designed for people who are eating healthily but still not losing weight properly. Most readers will not fall into this category and will achieve weight loss by omitting junk foods. This is aimed to take us past the plateau of no more weight loss even while eating good foods. Besides, we need our sour taste buds developed, not our sweet.

3.   **Why not dried fruit?** Just check the sugar content chart to find out why. They are loaded with sugar, concentrated sugar to be exact—definitely out!

4.   **Nuts are recommended for people with hypoglycemia, why aren't we encouraged to eat them?** Actually, most overeaters don't need any encouragement to eat nuts. They are concentrated sources of protein and also carbohydrates. In other words, they're great for others, but not for us, except in small amounts. Most overeaters just love endless handfuls of oily roasted and salted nuts. Really, one handful (without the oil) is a whole protein meal and if you find that you can eat just a few, then do so,

but a few is around three or four. My personal preference is for raw nuts, cheese, fruit and vegetables, but while eating this way I never lost weight. Too much of the right thing is still wrong, so until we have given God both our food and our appetite, then leave the nuts to the normal folks and the squirrels.

5. **Why is milk excluded?** Most reducing diets advise you to drink it. Actually, the calcium requirements are better met for abnormal carbohydrate metabolism through cottage cheese and cheese which has a low carbohydrate count. If you drink milk occasionally, try raw milk, since pasteurization kills valuable enzymes that occur in milk. Milk is high in carbohydrates. I don't believe that adults need milk because they can receive calcium from other sources. All the following foods provide almost the same amount of or more calcium than milk (those marked by an asterisk are good for people with abnormal carbohydrate metabolisms): almonds, american cheese*, cauliflower*, swiss cheese*, egg yolk*, filberts, gelatin (plain)*, haddock*, kale*, sardines*, shrimp*, sole*, turnip greens*, whitefish*. The following foods do not exceed the calcium found in milk, but are good sources of it: asparagus, bass, beets, cabbage greens, carrots, celery, coconut, eggs, flounder, whole wheat, grapefuit, herring, lettuce, okra, onions, oranges, parsnips, peanut butter, peas, potatoes, raspberries, rutabagas, salmon, shredded wheat, strawberries, sole, tangerines, turkey, turnips, walnuts. Again, this is not a complete list and many items would not be used for weight loss, but you see that you can provide calcium for your family and yourself without drinking so much milk. The dairy industry is big business today and many of us have been brainwashed into thinking we will perish without gallons of milk. One goat for one family is probably enough (ha ha).

For perfect health, we must have perfect digestion, assimilation and elimination. Diets which don't produce this are not right for us personally. Poisonous waste matter in the system is the result of taking more food than the body can assimilate or eliminate.

It is not always the amount of food that causes the problem, but wrong combinations and indigestible foods, like greasy and fried foods. Overeating or too-frequent eating produces a toxic state in the system and overtaxes the digestive organs, the food becomes impure and diseases of various kinds occur. It also produces excessive acid and causes the gastric mucous membrane to become congested. An excessive intake of food is much more common than a deficiency. When the bowels are full already, the second meal is compelled to lie in the stomach and sour. When this food putrefies, its poisons are absorbed back into the blood and consequently the whole system is poisoned. Overeating makes the work of the stomach, liver, kidneys and bowels much harder.

Half of what we eat keeps us alive, and the other half makes us sick. Disease does not normally gain a foothold in a healthy, properly-fed body. God's heart must hurt to see His people harm themselves with their own forks, when all we have to do is live "simply." The deceitful, dainty, junk foods need to be done away with, and it is we who must decide to offer to God not only our hearts, but our tastebuds, desires, appetites and forks as well. He will supply the supernatural power when we make that decision. He will never let us down. God will allow us to fail and fill our mouths with ice cream until all our teeth fall out, but He will also give us the self-control we need when we *ask* Him for it and believe that He alone has the power to change our tastebuds and help us to desire more of Him and less of food. Remember, He specializes in the impossible and His strength is made perfect in our weakness. He will take a weakness and turn it into a strength when we ask, believe and receive what He has for us.

Now, let's go into just some general rules concerning nutrition for health, which is different than nutrition for weight loss. Remember, nutrition for health varies according to your individual body's needs.

Many people ask me, "How did you get your family to eat right?" I answer, "I threatened them with starvation!" Of course, I'm joking. Actually I began first by cutting down on sugar and used honey occasionally. Then, I *quit* buying sugar. This must be done with your husband's consent (but not your kids')! If your family is addicted to sugar foods they'll go buy their own at the store—you can't be with them every minute, but you can set the right example. A study of Dr. Yudkin's book, *Sweet & Dangerous*, would be helpful.

Begin gradually to incorporate nutritious foods in your menus and eventually your family will get on the bandwagon, Lord willing. Everybody wants to be healthy! They'll feel the difference too! If you don't have junk food in the house—guess what?—no one can eat it! Provide good snacks for them. Include fresh fruits, vegetables, nuts, milk, juices and the like. Also experiment with honey-sweetened baked goods (if it's not too great a temptation for you). We have a cookbook that includes some excellent recipes that children and husbands love, and best of all—they're good for them!

But, for sure, the best way to begin nutritious eating is to eliminate bad foods from your diet. Let's look at some of the worst culprits. Coffee—Dr. Dorian Paskowitz tells us that the A.M.A. has labeled coffee as a drug and not a food. Five or more cups a day can lead to heart attacks. Coffee is high in caffeine which is addictive and destructive of B-vitamins. When you give it up, be ready for some withdrawal symptoms, like headache (severe migraines in some cases), nausea, vomiting (rare), diarrhea, nervousness, irritability and so on. "Look up, for your redemption draweth nigh." All tests have their beginning and their end, and so will this one!

Decaffeinated Coffee—Some of the substances used to decaffeinate coffee are more harmful than the caffeine itself.

Cereal Coffees—These are not harmful to health and can be used in moderation. But they do have a carbohydrate content. If you can drink them and handle the carbohydrates, then do so.

Tea—This refers to regular commercial tea, not herb teas like comfrey leaf, alfalfa, or camomile. Commercial tea contains approximately half the caffeine that coffee does, depending on how strong you make it. It also contains tannic acid, which can be harmful to health as well.

Soft Drinks—Diet and regular soft drinks can have from two to five times as much caffeine as coffee. What does a person do? No coffee, no tea, no pop! What's to drink? As Dr. Paskowitz said, "Well, water is nice." That's not what we wanted to hear, right? Water is nice, and we should drink more pure water, but relax. God doesn't rip things away from us, He waits until we give them up to Him first. I switched from coffee to tea to diet pop, and then to herb tea. It took about two years. Coffee was the hardest! I still drink tea occasionally. If you must have diet soda, choose the non-cola variety. Check the label for caffeine. You'll really feel a lot better, eventually, if not at first.

Sugar—Try to eliminate table sugar from your diet altogether. See what leading scientists and nutritionists have to say about the effects of sugar on your physical and mental health. They are staggering. Don't listen to the sugar industry's advertising claims. They want to sell sugar. Let the Holy Spirit direct you. You can consume two cups of sugar a day without ever eating a crystal of table sugar. Fruits and vegetables are loaded with natural sugars—the only sugars you need for high energy.

Dr. John Yudkin explains: 1) Our bodies do not need sugar; all our nutritional needs can be met in full without having to take a single spoonful of white, brown or raw sugar on its own or added to any food or drink. 2) If only a fraction of what is already known about the deleterious effects of sugar was shown to be true about any other food additive, that additive would promptly be banned by the Food and Drug Administration!

Did you know that one-fifth of all calories consumed is in sugar foods? Check those labels. Sugar is in almost every processed, refined or prepared food you buy! An average person will consume about 120 pounds of sugar per year. We eat twenty times as much as our ancestors did. Sugar has no nutritional value at all—no vitamins, no minerals, nothing. That's why it's pure. Sugar is advertised as a source of "quick energy." That's because it's like alcohol; it passes directly from the stomach into the bloodstream. Pep pills give you quick energy, too, but are they beneficial for you? The harm sugar does far outweighs any benefit it might bring in terms of momentary energy. Besides, people don't eat sweets because they want energy, but because they like the taste.

According to J. I. Rodale, well-known nutritionist and author, millions are suffering from low blood sugar (hypoglycemia) and diabetes (hyperglycemia) because of a diet high in sugar and refined foods. Tests have been made on groups of hyperactive and problem children. All sugar (including that in refined and prepared food) was omitted from their diet and after a while they began to behave quite normally. They were healthier and had fewer colds and infections. When put back on sugar foods, they reverted to their old behavior. Symptoms of low blood sugar in children are overeating, loss of memory, nightmares, bedwetting, sleepwalking, dullness, mental fatigue, indifference, and much more. These studies don't end with children—sugar affects adults too! Mr. Rodale believes there is a direct relation between low blood sugar (eating too much sugar) and criminality! Numerous studies were made on criminals, and most were big sugar eaters.

Did you know that none of the brown sugars contain any worthwhile amount of nutrients? Raw sugar is just "dirty sugar" and can't be considered a source of nutrients. The only benefit to eating brown or raw sugar is that they are not quite as palatable and you don't use as much, so the harmful effects are not as bad!

How can you change your family's eating habits?

1. Check all the labels! Don't buy packaged foods that contain sugar unless it is fifth or below on the label. (Packaged salad dressing mixes are all right because, when they are prepared, the sugar content is diluted a lot.)
2. Sit down and think of all the things God made that your family likes or might like. Make a list! Now start incorporating these foods into as many meals as you can! Instead of having bags of cookies, chips and empty calories, try to buy fresh fruits (or unsweetened or light syrup canned ones), nuts (all kinds) and fresh vegetables.
3. If they do crave sweets, try experimenting with your recipes by using honey instead of sugar, or at least part of each.

Sugar is especially destructive to the beauty of skin. Refined sugars not only falsely satisfy our appetite and fill us with "foodless" foods, but they feed bacteria that are always very active in undernourished skin. The first thing that skin doctors take away from afflicted patients is refined sugar and foods that contain significant quantities of sugar—ice cream, pastries, candy and soft drinks.

Did you know that sugar is added to table salt? Read the label. It has "dextrose" (sugar). Gasp! Sea salt is available at health stores and I recommend it in preference to the other type.

White Flour—When teaching on bleached flour, I often ask someone in the audience who's wearing white how they keep their whites bright—what makes them stay white? They answer "by bleaching them." That's the same way they get the white flour, by bleaching it. No, not with Clorox, but with a bleach that does the same thing. If you can eat flour (bread, etc.) without gaining weight, then get genuine whole wheat (don't be fooled by brown-colored bread). What they do to bread is a crime (or should be). Egg bread can have as little as one-tenth of an egg per loaf (read *The Great American Food Hoax*). Real bread (read *Health Wise*) should definitely not be one of the "soft guys." A firm, heavy, whole-grain loaf is the best—no preservatives. When we first tried a seven-grain loaf, the kids said that it tasted like bugs popping in their mouths, but now they often ask for it. Most of us haven't been used to chewing anything except gum and candy bars. It takes time to change eating habits. (For more on wheat, see the section on wheat germ).

Salt—Table salt is sodium chloride. The nutritional experts tell us that salt is a preservative but nowadays it is considered a necessity to everyday eating. Regular table salt is composed of insoluble inorganic elements. Many health problems can be traced to excessive salt in the diet. Salt is necessary in the generation and functions of digestive fluids in the system. Without salt, good digestion is impossible. But table salt is not the source of the sodium our bodies need. In commercial production of table salt, extremely high temperatures are used, around 1,500 degrees F. to solidify the salt, and then additives and adulterants are included to coat the crystals and make them "pourable." Dextrose (sugar) is one of the additives. If salt must be used, health authorities recommend either sea salt or rock salt, in small quantities. Table salt is indigestible, but God has provided sodium in the following foods: tomatoes, asparagus, celery, spinach, kale, radishes, turnips, carrots, lettuce, strawberries, and many others.

"I'd like to speak to you about . . . regularity." Sound familiar? It should. Americans spent a fortune last year on

laxatives, but no one wants to talk about the problem. I've taught many classes on weight loss, controlled eating and nutrition, and I would guess that from the response to this subject, at least seven out of every ten people who attend suffer from constipation. If you have this problem, then suffer is exactly what you do, not only from headaches, upset stomach, abdominal cramps, and hemorrhoids, but also from the gnawing feeling that "something's gone wrong." To quote Dr. David Reuben, "One of the greatest risks a human being can take is to allow the remnants of his food, that is fecal-end products, to remain in contact with the lining of his colon for three and four days at a time. And, that's exactly what ninety-nine percent of Americans and others who eat a 'modern diet' do, and at the end of their digestive tract they are harboring a 'time bomb.' This is what the researchers in laboratories around the world have found" (*The Save-Your-Life Diet*, p. 27).

Roughage has a lot to do with healthy, regular elimination and in the United States ninety per cent of the roughage is removed from over 11,000 processed foods. Could this be why the incidence of colon cancer in the U.S. is nine hundred per cent greater than that of Nigeria and thirteen hundred per cent greater than Uganda, two countries which have high-roughage diets.

The colon is not a cement septic tank built to hold sewage, it is instead a living organism which absorbs a wide variety of potent chemicals from the feces it contains. The longer the waste is in contact with the colon, the greater the putrefaction and serious consequences. Dr. Reuben indicates "There is evidence that refined sugar alters the dominant type of bacteria present in the colon and increases the possibility of colon and rectal cancer. It also may contribute to the elevation of blood cholesterol" (p. 88, from M.J. Hill, et al., "Bacteriology and Aetiology of Cancer of the Large Bowel," 1971, *LANCET* 1:95-99).

Since laxatives are habit forming, and no one recommends taking a daily enema, what should we do? Fiber in diet is extremely important, but again many are not able to lose weight on a diet rich in fiber, regardless of what the experts say. For this reason we give the following hints that have helped many.

1. One or two tablespoons of fresh wheat germ daily. (See section on wheat germ.) This may be taken in cereal, eggs, juice, milk or just eaten plain. It should taste sweet and not bitter; if bitter, discard. It's rancid.

2. Add bran to your diet. The amount will depend on your own system. One or two tablespoons daily is usually enough. Regularity will tell you when you've had enough. Eat it as you would wheat germ, or put in soups and stews. You can eat it dry, but be sure to drink a lot of liquid, or you'll compound the problem.

3. Warm or hot water upon arising with the juice of a fresh lemon in it. Don't ask me why it works, it just does. Also, many just drink a full glass of water and this does the trick.

4. Sure Fire Remedy! Last Resort! (It works!) This is high in calories and carbohydrates, but if you've got the problem of extreme constipation, then it's worth it. Cut out other foods and take this just before bedtime.
½ c. plain yogurt
1 or 2 T. wheat germ or bran
2-3 stewed prunes
Mix until prunes are mashed throughout. (If you like, add a little uncooked honey for taste, but the prunes should be sweet enough.)

5. Herbs—Psalm 104:14, "and herbs for the service of all mankind." Herbs have been used, since time began, to

heal and restore. Gen. 1:11-12, 29, 2:5, 3:18 and many other verses refer to the fact that God intended man to use herbs. Many people (Christians included) think you're strange if you use herbs, but they think nothing of going to the drugstore and spending all kinds of money on laxatives, reducing pills, water pills, sleeping pills, breath mints, cough drops, etc. There are many helpful books out on herbs. Why not visit your health food store or book store and see what they have.

Wheat Germ—A fantastic food! Why is it so great? It's part of the wheat kernel which sprouts to make the new plant. Therefore it provides everything the new plant needs to sustain itself—protein, vitamins and minerals.

When wheat is milled into white flour, the rich and highly perishable wheat germ is removed. Eight hours after the wheat is cracked or milled, the germ loses its potency, so be sure to buy your wheat germ and whole wheat flour fresh at your health food store and not in the supermarket. I used to freeze my wheat germ, but I learned that this will not prevent it from becoming rancid, because fats don't freeze, they just solidify. For best results, buy what you need for seven days, and refrigerate it.

One-half cup of fresh wheat germ contains twenty-four grams of protein, as much as one-quarter pound of beef, four times as much as an egg and eight times as much as a slice of white bread. Only a few foods (liver, parsley and greens of various kinds) are richer in iron than wheat germ. Iron deficiency anemia is common in America and many people are taking iron medicines just because they eat white flour and thus avoid one of the best sources of iron. Wheat germ is also rich in minerals, like manganese, magnesium copper and potassium.

You can eat wheat germ and not gain weight, but if you eat whole-wheat bread, you put on weight. Wheat is a heavy carbohydrate. It builds fat, especially if eaten with meat and fatty foods. Many of us have become "wheat-logged" because of the devitalized processed foods we previously consumed.

The Menstrual Cycle—Did you know that half of the women who commit suicide do so during the week prior to the onset of their period? One doctor told his patient that, after examining some research statistics, he had begun to believe that women actually experience something like water on the brain during menstruation. Whether that's true or not, most women experience some degree of stress just prior to and during the time their uteri shed their linings.

When our bodies undergo stress—be it physical or emotional—they use up the B vitamins. Our diets are often deficient in one or more of them (there are more than a dozen of them) and, when that happens, we respond poorly to stress. Did I say poorly? Talk about touchy! It can really get frenzied—right, ladies?

So where do we get those good B vitamins? They're available—all or almost all of them—in bean sprouts, wheat germ, liver, and brewer's yeast, to name a few prevalent sources. By the way, that's why some doctors used to recommend beer for nursing mothers: the yeast made beer rich in B vitamins which are essential to good lactation. Sad to say, American brewers no longer use yeast in their recipes.

Then, of course, there are B-vitamin tablets. But beware of the synthetic sorts. I have a very dear friend whose little girl suffered from cancer of the kidney and, in turn, of the liver. The surgeon successfully removed both tumors and told the parents that he strongly suspected that they were caused by the synthetic vitamins she had been taking. They were—as are all synthetic vitamins—derived from coal tar, a known cancer producer. Postscript: the little girl is alive and healthy today. Praise the Lord!

Another aid for this time of the month is Vitamin C (500-1,000 mg. per day)—natural only. This, along with the B complex, especially helps during the menstrual cycles, but don't expect them to help unless you take them daily during the entire month. If you're really brave and want a drink that is Vitamin C and iron-packed, try ten ounces of V-8 juice and a cup or more of parsley liquefied in your blender. We call it "Swamp Drink." It may not look terrific, but it really works!

Licorice root, which is available as a powder or in capsules, has been successfully used by some doctors to treat women who suffer from a lack of estrogen (a hormone). These women and girls had unusually long and heavy menstrual cycles. After taking licorice root, one forty-three-year-old woman said, "I've had a normal period for the first time in my life." A licorice candy made with honey was also used in less severe cases with good results. Possibly the reason that it's been reported that licorice causes headaches, high blood pressure, etc. is because God made it to be a medicine, not a candy. Even the women being treated for female problems were told to take only three capsules per day.

Many have found that taking a good multi-vitamin and mineral tablet, made them feel like a new person. Ninety per cent of all overweight people are anemic; overweight but underfed. You can be fat and still be starving nutritionally.

Having said all this, let's go back and remember that since we are removing food from its pedestal and no longer letting it be a god to us, we should not let nutrition take its place. Good nutrition, yes, but not as a god to be worshiped! Nutritionists don't have all the answers, but our true God does. He is the giver and we the receiver. The simple rule of taking foods as near their natural state as possible or desirable will cure a multitude of questions. Don't be either a food worshiper or a nutrition worshiper; just use good sense!

God doesn't have anything against good food. I understand He is planning a wedding feast for us. I am sure it will be the best food we have ever eaten.

So my parting word to you: be adventurous on the side of good, interesting eating, with the limits of good health placed on it. Don't eat so as to fatten, but do find new ways, new recipes, interesting ways to serve food so that it will be satisfying to the body. While you look for recipes to make your allowed foods more palatable and interesting, you will find some that will become a part of your life. Keep on looking for foods that you can enjoy without becoming enslaved again to the fatteners, the stupefying addictive foods, the killers.

As your body loses its burden and becomes more energetic, look for ways to expend that energy other than tripping to the market for groceries. Ask God for "new paths to live in."

15 Not by Bread Alone

I have esteemed the words of the Lord more than my necessary food. Job 23:12

You will stand or fall on what you do with this chapter. When we plan our victories by the truth and power of God's word, we cannot fail, because God says "I will watch over my word to perform it . . ." (Jer. 1:12). Never underestimate the power of God's word! "Is not my word as the hammer that breaks the rock in pieces . . ." (Jer. 23:29). The results of planting and nurturing spiritual seed are certain and foreordained. *Victory is the product of a well-fed spirit and application of the word of God.*

Getting alone with God in the morning to set your will toward your new life style will be the most important thing you do all day. In God lies the power to overcome the world, the flesh, and the devil. This means temptations, your own bad training and slipshod habits, and all those clever traps the world sets to catch us in our weaknesses.

There is only one way to fatten the spirit: feed it! There is only one way to build a relationship with God the Father: through a two-way conversation. There is only one way to overcome compulsive eating: spiritual discipline. There is only one way to acquire spiritual maturity: read the textbook.

Any effort toward betterment that stems from the needs and goals of the flesh is doomed to failure; it can only tear you down and cause you to go back to it always. "For the mind set on the flesh is death, but the mind set on the Spirit is life and peace, because the mind set on the flesh is hostile toward God, for it does not subject itself to the law of God, for it is not even able to do so" (Rom. 8:6, 7 NAS). The result of seeking the gifts and not the giver never works, for the attempt strengthens us in selfishness and lusts of the flesh; we are then out of harmony with our creator and our purpose is defeated. "The world will pass away and all the lusts thereof . . . but he that does the will of God abideth forever" (I John 2:17).

Did that rascal, Satan, just whisper in your ear, "Yeah, that sounds good, but you've read the Bible before and it didn't do all this for you!" That may be so, but we have declared a new day unto the Lord. In the past some of the links in the chain were left out; now we are working together to add the missing links. In the past, we had blind spots where the deceiver could work undetected, but now that spot is being exposed to the truth. We are sharing this victory road together for the very purpose of being aware of the "whole counsel of God." I did a lot of stumbling, finding these truths by trial and error, by failure and success, by sheer determination and the help of many people. You can benefit by my mistakes and take a straighter path!

In the past, we tried to lose weight using our own self-discipline and will power, and we failed often because our equipment was defective. We struggled with calories, carbohydrates, fleshy cravings, and we used the wrong motives and had the wrong perspectives. No wonder we lost the battle! But now we have made the right decision and have looked to the right source for help. Get thee behind me, Satan!

For too long we have been gluttons at the table, and have done our fasting on the word of God. Now we put that the other way around. Standing on the word of God and making it a part of your life is the key to overcoming; that is the way Jesus did it. When temptation comes (and it will), you will be prepared for it. Also, the word contains healing for the spiritual part of your eating problem. Without this part, your healing is incomplete.

Jesus went before us as an overcomer, and in some mysterious way that we cannot explain, He imparts the power of His resurrection triumph to us. Theologians call it our "mystical union with Christ." The word describes it thus: "I am crucified with Christ, nevertheless I live: yet not I, but Christ liveth in me, and the life which I now live in the flesh, I live by the faith of the son of God, who loved me, and gave himself for me" (Gal. 2:20). We open ourselves to what God has for us, not just because we want to lose weight, nor even because we want power in our lives; we do it because the Lord Jesus wanted it for us. This is seeking the giver and not the gifts. "For the LORD God is a sun and a shield; the LORD will give grace and glory; no good thing will he withhold from them that walk uprightly" (Psalm 84:11). We accept and walk uprightly only as we live by faith, and this faith is imparted through the word; we are washed and cleansed by the word so that we can do the impossible. We are out to gain mastery over a deep-seated problem, and we can succeed because we know where to get "grace and glory."

The weapons of our warfare are not carnal, but spiritual (II Cor. 10:4). They are hidden in the heart (Psalm 119:11). This means that we will read, ponder, and memorize the Scriptures. We will keep them by us and have them ready. When Satan comes along, and he will, won't he be surprised? And the

Scriptures are more than a sword, they inspire, teach, comfort, encourage, rebuke, chasten, exhort, and fill with blessings the one who searches them. "All Scripture is inspired by God and is profitable for teaching, for reproof, for correction, for training in righteousness, that the man of God may be adequate, equipped for every good work" (II Tim. 3:16, 17).

The food in the house of the Lady Wisdom is the word of God, and it is the food that benefits. There are so many benefits that we cannot name them all! The following is a sample of the feast that is waiting for you and the benefits you will receive. The word of God . . .

cleanses. "Now are ye clean through the word I have spoken unto you" (John 15:3). "If we confess our sins, He is faithful and righteous to forgive us our sins and to cleanse us from all unrighteousness" (I John 1:9). The way to stay clean is to confess and repent daily; this is a healthy and wholesome way to live. Satan really gets his licks in here, for he insists that *you* have to qualify personally before God will accept you, and of course you can never make it, so you feel defeated. Here is where that bank account comes in—Jesus has imputed His own righteousness to you, and it is yours for believing it!

teaches. "Learn of me, for I am meek and lowly . . ." (Matt. 11:29). Jesus is saying that He has lived here where you are and He can counsel you as no one else can. He came as the humblest of men on purpose so He could reach all; no one is excluded. All He asks is that you believe Him, and you demonstrate this belief when you learn of Him.

guides. "But when He, the Spirit of Truth comes, He will guide you into all truth . . ." (John 16:13). In addition to that, "The Holy Spirit will also bring all things to your remembrance" (John 14:26) and you can rely on Him to keep you in remembrance of your Prayer of Agreement and the weapons you need, as well as the comforts and guidance you will need daily. You just give it some "input" and He will work it through you for good.

satisfies. "We have eaten and not been satisfied, and there is still hunger in our inward parts" (Micah 6:14). That deep-down craving that we tried to satisfy with earthly food—unsuccessfully—will be satisfied with spiritual food. The "unseen" input will get the job done and work out in tangible benefits. "All my springs are in thee" (Psalm 87:7). Earthly food can never feed insecurity, anxiety, etc. It was designed to feed only the physical body. Only spiritual food will feed the spirit.

yields self-control. His presence within, which comes only through spiritual input, accomplishes the fruit of the spirit: love, joy, peace, patience, kindness, goodness, faithfulness, gentleness, self-control . . . (Gal. 5:22, 23). My daughter Christa told me that all fruit is a covering to protect the seed that was planted (they learn these things in school!). His presence in us is the seed. With water from the living water of His word, warmth and quickening by the Holy Spirit, the nurture of faith, the seed will flower and mature in due season to give up the fruit that was foreordained. As God's Spirit is allowed growth room within you, it will bring the body under subjection, and *that's the victory.*

reproves. Those of us who are not well-disciplined will have to accept some reproof from God's word. "Whoever loves discipline loves knowledge, but he who hates reproof is stupid" (Prov. 12:1). That's laying it on the line!

comforts. "Blessed be the God and Father of our Lord Jesus Christ, the Father of sympathy . . . and the God of every comfort and consolation and encouragement, who consoles and comforts and encourages us in every trouble (calamity and affliction) so that we may also be able to console . . . those who are in any kind of trouble or distress, with the consolation . . . with which we ourselves are consoled and comforted and encouraged by God" (II Cor. 1:3, 4 Ampl).

yields joy. "A happy heart is a good medicine and a cheerful mind works healing, but a broken spirit dries the bones" (Prov.

17:22). Only a Christian has the ingredients of joy so that he can sing and shout praises to God at midnight while he is chained to the wall of a dank prison cell (Acts 16:25). Paul and Silas were so full of the joy of the Lord that their immediate circumstances had little effect on them; they were plugged into the power source and joy had to result regardless of where they were at the moment. Don't let Satan tell you that you will have to wait until you have gained the goal before you can have joy—no! That is a lie. Accept the joy now; you will need it for strength to get to the goal. "The joy of the Lord is my strength" (Neh. 8:10). It is one of the mysteries of the gospel that, even though we have not "arrived yet," we can pretend that we have! We have the benefits of arrival while we are still traveling the road. We need those benefits *now* to endure to the end where the overcomer's crown awaits. God provided for this; we can think and act the victory now by accepting His joy, and this is only possible through God's word; it was designed to infuse joy.

overcomes temptation. The Scriptures give guidance through temptation. "Watch and pray that you may not enter into temptation; the spirit indeed is willing, but the flesh is weak" (Matt. 26:41). The Scriptures strengthen the willing spirit so that it is stronger than the weak flesh. "For no temptation—no trial regarded as enticing to sin (no matter how it comes or where it leads)—has overtaken you and laid hold on you that is not common to man—that is, no temptation or trial has come to you that is beyond human resistance and that is not adjusted and adapted and belonging to human experience, and such as man can bear, but God is faithful (to His word and to His compassionate nature) and He can be trusted not to let you be tempted and tried . . . beyond your ability and strength of resistance and power to endure, but with the temptation He will always also provide the way out—the means of escape to a landing place—that you may be capable and strong and powerful patiently to bear up under it." That says it all! Many of us know the word of God, but we are not practiced at applying it. Bringing it out of spiritual limbo and putting it to use will be a practical and effective step to victory.

heals. The prophet Jeremiah spoke out against false prophets who "healed slightly" (6:14) and thus deceived God's people. As you read further in Jeremiah, you find that these prophets were "stealing" God's word from the people by substituting their own dreams and visions for God's word. Only God's word could heal thoroughly. A slight healing is worse than no healing at all, because the people think they are all right when they are not. The same principle is found in Rev. 3:15—it is dangerous to be lukewarm, because you have a little warmth left and are not aware of your need. God would prefer that you be cold rather than lukewarm, because then you are aware of need. So with a slight healing; the unsolved sickness festers beneath the thin crust of a slight healing, and will eventually break forth worse than ever (if it doesn't kill you first). In a way, we fatties can be glad that our need is out where it shows. We will have to find a thorough healing to solve our problem. With a complete healing, we won't have to wrestle with our problem all our lives; we can go on to better things. That is good news!

The world is full of books that tell you how to get thin, but most fail because they offer only a slight healing. Only the word of God can penetrate and heal from inside out. Only a path that takes in the spiritual need of God's people will offer a complete healing. Easy formulas and cliches have an opposite effect on the sufferer than the one intended: they can't cope, so they repress their problem in the face of these "easy-does-it" philosophies. Then they are worse off than ever. But the washing of God's word has a different effect; it exhorts in such a way as to expose truth. It gives hope because when we confess the sin that is revealed by that truth there is forgiveness and healing begins from the inside out. The healing is stringent and yet gentle, because God gives strength and comfort and hope even while He purges and convicts. What a combination for victory!

changes our wanter. The Greeks had a school of philosophy which taught that satisfying the physical appetite was the highest aim of man. They worshiped their stomachs, pleasure was their standard of living, and appetite was their god. Paul alluded to them in Phil. 3:18, 19: "For many walk, of whom I often told you, and now tell you even weeping, that they are enemies of the cross of Christ, whose end is destruction, whose god is their appetite, and whose glory is in their shame, who set their minds on earthly things." Compare their attitude with that of restored Israel in Isa. 26:8: "In the way of thy judgments, O Lord, have we waited for thee; the desire of our soul is to thy name, and to the remembrance of thee." Compare it also with the attitude of David in Psalm 73:25, "Whom have I in heaven but Thee? And besides Thee, I desire nothing on earth." And throughout Psalm 119 the psalmist reaffirms his desire: "I shall delight in Thy commandments, which I love . . . O how I love Thy law! It is my meditation all the day . . . Thy word is a lamp to my feet, and a light to my path." David was beloved of the Lord, the apple of His eye, not so much because he never did wrong, but because of his beautiful attitude. And he acquired that attitude through his meditation in God's precepts. "Thy law is my delight; let my soul live that it may praise thee" (Psalm 119:174).

provides skill, armor, weapons. If someone gave me a gun right this minute and pushed me into a situation where I had to use it or be killed, I'd be a nervous wreck. The only time in my life that I fired a gun—it was a shotgun—I blew myself into a ditch. I had never practiced with it and didn't know a thing about how to use it except to pull the trigger. If you don't practice with the word of God, you can't expect it to work for you because you won't know how to work it. The way to gain skill is to *use* it, ". . . even those who by reason of *use* have their senses exercised to discern both good and evil" (Heb. 5:14).

Without armor, you will get scuffed up in the battle, and may even lose it. Christians everywhere live beneath their inheritance when they fail in this. Don't go out of your house without putting on the armor of God. Don't trust yourself in the grocery store or the kitchen without the armor of God. Don't eat a meal without it. "And, finally, brethren, put on the whole armor of God that ye may be able to stand against the wiles of the devil" (Eph. 6:10; also read verses 11 and 17!)

Jesus overcame by letting his spiritual life grow in all the depth and dimension available to sons of God. He pondered and expounded the Scriptures, and He met Satan on the same grounds as you and I, using the weapons that are available to us. Keep Scripture cards on your table, in your purse or pocket, posted above the sink and any place else you think they'll be handy. They are not only spiritual food but convenient weapons right on the scene of battle.

leads to victory. Faith is the victory that overcomes the world (I John 5:4, 5) and our faith grows as we absorb the message of the Bible. "He that overcomes shall inherit all these things, and I will be his God and he will be My son" (Rev. 21:7). "He who overcomes shall thus be clothed in white garments; and I will not erase his name from the book of life, and I will confess his name before my Father, and before his angels" (Rev. 3:5). "Blessed is the man who perseveres under trial; for once he has been approved, he will receive the crown of life, which the Lord has promised to those who love Him" (James 1:12). If we are "in Christ" we can't help going where He is going, and He has already arrived at victory. If you "put on" something, that means you wear it, you get inside it. Now if you put on a garment, it will have to go with you wherever you go; it has no choice. But if you put on the Lord Jesus Christ, you will go with Him, for He has already gone, and you will have no choice except to go along. "But put on the Lord Jesus Christ, and make no provision for the flesh in regard to its lusts" (Rom. 13:14). Put on Christ, and victory is a sure thing, because He already has it!

If we truly love Him, we show it by keeping His commands (John 14:15 and 21). One of His commands was to "learn of Me." As we learn, we will put Him on as the word exhorts, and find ourselves conforming to His image and going along with Him.

One word of exhortation on *how* to read the Scriptures. It is unfortunately true that some people read the Bible and it doesn't appear to do much to change them. This is because they read dutifully, with ears that were pre-trained to hear only certain things. Often they see only through eyes that are negative and legalistic, or through a self-centeredness that excludes anything that would open eyes and convict and heal. Pre-programming makes the ears dull. Ask for the Spirit of Truth so you can zero in on all God has for you. Read with honesty and expectancy.

If it seems like a duty to read the Bible daily, that is merely proof of how badly trained our flesh is. David truly delighted in God's word, and it will grow to be your delight. Only through His word will God's thoughts penetrate our thoughts until they become part of our actions. It will set up its own craving within you, so that you will find yourself hungering and thirsting for "righteousness." Those of us who have found earthly food a snare will find freedom from such bondage when we feed our spirits with proper food.

Open yourself to retraining and reprogramming in God's word. It will make you aware of how the world has manipulated and trained your mind, and the truth will set you free. Read carefully, not to find proof for notions you already had, but to discover new notions! God's merest thought is above our highest thought, and His word pulls us upward with a beneficial effect.

Satan has had a heyday with our weaknesses because he has a planned program of brainwashing. His ways are popular with the world because they have never learned to think differently, but when we get into the word we will see what really is popular—not necessarily with the majority but with the mightiest! We will rebuke and repudiate the brainwashing of Satan's world as we fill our minds with something better.

Begin to "store up" the right kind of memories; you will need them for the bad days. There are certain to be moments when you will wish you had never begun your program of change. The Israelites were having one of those days out on the desert, and they got so mad they insulted God. "Would that we had died by the hand of the LORD in the land of Egypt, when we sat by the fleshpots and ate bread to the full; for you have brought us out into this wilderness to kill us with hunger" (Exod. 16:3). They were mad and hungry, and sadly out of condition for life on the desert. They didn't mind being dead as much as being separated from their fleshpots! They forgot all about the horrid bondage that went with the fleshpots of Egypt, and they were willing to trade their precious freedom for food!

David showed us a better way. When he was in the wilderness, he remembered what God had done for him in the past, and he looked forward to what God would do for him in the future. "Because thou hast been my help, therefore in the shadow of thy wings will I rejoice" (Psalm 63:7). He too was in a dry and weary land where there was no water, but he recalled God's power and glory, he remembered God's lovingkindness and thought it better than life (verse 3), therefore he sang "My lips will praise Thee, So I will bless Thee as long as I live; I will lift up my hands in Thy name" (vv. 3, 4). His secret is found in verses 6 and 8: "I remember Thee on my bed, I meditate on Thee in the night watches. My soul clings to Thee. . . ." David meditated on the word of God; he composed songs of praise; he loved God's laws and precepts.

135

If you have trouble acquiring the habit of Scripture reading, try the "principle of the will" again. Set your will to be made willing. Tell God so. Confess your sin of carelessness and spiritual deadness; ask His forgiveness, healing, and restoration. Ask Him to fill you with hunger and thirst for His word. Jesus has "food to eat of which you do not know" (John 4:32), and when you begin to know it, you will like it. The self-indulgent flesh may rebel at first, and the old "familiar food" that caused the damage may seem more exciting to your body than the food which it does not yet know. But God's word is exciting and satisfying, and it will grow to be your daily meat and drink.

This period of training will take some discipline, to be sure. Satan has gained a hold on us and it must be broken with our determination to be wise. In the past, we spent plenty of time planning good things to eat. Now we need to spend some time planning our way of escape. Freedom awaits, and it is worth the effort! We need to put to death the deeds of the flesh, which are promoted by the cravings of our bodies (Rom. 8:12, 13). The job gets done by the Spirit, who belongs to the children of God!

Recently I visited Alcatraz prison in San Francisco Bay. It is empty of inmates now and tourists can see the interior of this grim prison where escape was almost impossible. Yet three men did escape. They may have perished in the waters of the bay, but they have never been found. They burrowed a tunnel out of Alcatraz with spoons, working by night for eleven long months. They really wanted out! They planned carefully, they worked at it, and they got out.

We have something much better than a spoon to dig our way out of our prison! We have the Spirit of God and assurance of victory. If we want out, we can get out.

There are many Scriptures "just for you," and yours is the adventure of finding them. Here is a list to look up and enjoy, for a starter, and there are many more!

Isa. 35:4	I Cor. 3:16	Matt. 26:41
Lam. 3:40, 41	I Cor. 6:12, 13, 20	John 8:32
Prov. 23:1-3	I Cor. 9:25-27	Rom. 6:13, 8:11, 12
Prov. 11:30	I Cor. 10:13, 14	Phil. 1:29
Zech. 4:6	II Cor. 2:14	Phil. 4:12, 14
Eph. 6:10-17	I Tim. 6:11, 12	Heb. 4:12
Eph. 3:20	*I Tim. 1:7 (see Ampl)	
James 5:16	II Tim. 2:3, 4	Heb. 10:24, 25, 26
I Pet. 1:6, 7	I Thess. 5:14	Heb. 12:3, 11

I highly recommend that you read in the modern translations. The New American Standard is an accurate and easily understood translation. The Amplified gives help with many verses.

We begin and end with the Word. We search it, believe it, live by it, and furnish it a dwelling place, a house to live in, richly! We experience the new birth, we put on the new self, we practice the new life, and love moves in. Before we know it, we wake up one morning and find ourselves Christian overcomers. "And now I commend you to God and to the word of His grace, which is able to build you up and to give you the inheritance among all those who are sanctified" (Acts 20:32).

Appendixes

Repair Kit
Remember that the process of change is gradual. Try not to
expect too much too soon. The appetite will change, and as
weight is lost, the body will become more energetic. You will
find you have more time for the things that count. But there
will be times when you seem to hit a snag, or at least a plateau,
and I would like to share some of the answers that I found to this
problem by trial and error. First try to determine what went
wrong and then find the answer in God's word. These sugges-
tions might help:

1. *Out of harmony.* The Greek word that means "agreement"
    is *harmonia* from which we derive our English word har-

you have agreed not to eat desserts, and you continue to make them, you are not acting in harmony; something is out of tune. But if your actions are in agreement with your spirit, you are not only "hoping" for victory, but *agreeing* to it!

2. *Wrong name.* Did you get suddenly proud and think it was *you* who was sending Satan on his way? You have no power over the enemy; only Jesus has defeated him and only His name carries any weight with this prince of the power of the air.

3. *Strife in your life.* Disunity, or strife drains away your power. The apostles couldn't cast out a certain demon after strife. There was a hindrance. Remember the time you had been having a big fight, then it was time to go to church and you really couldn't get anything out of the service? Strife hinders. Find a place of prayer, let God's word do a healing work, then get together and mend the rift.

4. *Wrong information.* Do you still secretly feel that you're a special case and God's word doesn't apply to you? What does God have to say about your situation? If you find it convicts you, confess your wrongs quickly. Be quick to repent and take your stand on the rock of victory, Christ Jesus.

5. *You've let defeat linger.* If you fell into defeat, the only real loss is when you stay there. Get up and polish your weapons! You are still alive, and the victory has been announced. It *belongs* to you and failure cannot change that. Get up and claim it—don't let that lying one tell you that all is lost! He is the liar and Christ is the Truth, and

mony. You must harmonize your spirit, soul, and body. If Christ has told us that we can do all things through Him who strengthens us.

6. *You broke your agreement willfully.* So what? If you've broken your agreement, you are still bound to deal with your situation. It doesn't nullify your agreement to have it broken, whether it was once or many times, because the blood of Jesus continues to cleanse you as you confess and repent. You agreed to *have* self-control and you just keep on until you get it. Self-control is a fruit, and fruits have to grow. Give yourself time; don't chop yourself down before you have time to grow.

If your battles are being lost more often than they are being won, the solution is to ask God to tell you why. He just loves to do it! I had to ask Him to "dig me a new ear" as my old one was all plugged up with pride and self-righteousness. So ask, listen, and get ready for a feast for the soul, for "he who is able to hear, let him listen to and heed what the Spirit says to the church. To him who overcomes I give to eat of the manna that is hidden . . ." (Rev. 2:17).

When you feel that you are slipping even a little, be quick to join in agreement with a prayer partner for the victory; Jesus assures us that where two or three are gathered together in His name, He is in their midst (Matt. 20:20). Satan works overtime to keep people from agreeing, because it is such an effective weapon.

"And whatever you do, no matter what it is in word or deed, do everything in the name of the Lord Jesus and in dependence upon his person, giving praise to God the Father through him" (Col. 3:17 Ampl). Victory by His power will set praises on our lips and a song in our hearts and joy in our spirits.

More of Jesus, Less of Me

Testimonies by a Few of Those
Who Have Attended PACE-Weigh Seminars

"Since I began to eat properly and nutritiously, I've had a complete turnabout in living! After I decided to prepare well-balanced meals for my family, I began to notice that my children became more well-behaved. I feel great and am much happier about being a wife and mother."

Geri Anderson (56 lbs. lost)
Vista, California

"I lost fifty-two pounds after I attended PACE-Weigh classes and began to apply God's word to my life. I had previously tried many diets, pills, and exercises, but I had never lost more than a few pounds—which I inevitably gained back, plus a few more. I never had the willpower to see it through.

"But now I've learned that God has that power and has promised to help me through my temptations. By His power I have overcome not only my eating but many other obstacles to my daily walk with Jesus. I began to accept the Scriptures and the food plan with the same sense of helpless dependence that I accepted my salvation initially. When I fall, I repent, ask the Lord's forgiveness and move on, assured that His blood is sufficient for my sin and that there is nothing I can add to it. That's what I do whenever I cheat on my diet. I've stopped making excuses. I no longer give up and throw out my agreement. I praise God that He loves me and wants me to be an overcomer in every aspect of my life."

Minnie Portillo
San Diego, California

"After I attended PACE-Weigh classes for four months, I lost thirty-five pounds and went from a size eighteen to a twelve. I could hardly believe it! For twelve years I had tried one diet after another without success. My heavy eating began

142

in my teen years in a vain effort to deal with depression. As I grew older I loved to cook and I lived to eat! But now I have learned to face my depression and heal my hurts with the word of God and the name of Jesus Christ. He has given me a new life style that includes discipline. Now I feel lifted up rather than depressed. I've given Jesus full control of my life and I thank Him for everything He's done for me."

Ann MacFarlane
Poway, California

"I am so grateful to God for PACE-Weigh. Through it He has helped me to become free to obey Him in my eating. I signed the Prayer of Agreement and my husband signed it too. Boy, did that ever make a powerful impact on me! Joan helped me to relate this commitment to my spiritual commitment. And God also used her to help me see that I had not accepted myself as much as I thought I had. Praise the Lord!"

Carol Beard (15 lbs. lost)
Santee, California

"I was a human garbage disposal, but I never weighed more than 152 pounds because I would gorge myself and then retreat fearfully into a fast. I did it time and again, and endured real suffering for it. Praise God, I learned how to get free of that horrible yo-yo syndrome through the teachings of PACE-Weigh. I saw that the foods I loved—cakes, cookies, starches—were worthless and even harmful. God has helped me and now, instead of sweets, I actually enjoy natural foods like fruits and vegetables. God had waited patiently while I tried the pills and fad diets, until I was desperate enough to turn to Him. I finally gave up and let Him show me His way. Praise God!"

Pat Helps

"PACE-Weigh helped me realize I wasn't all alone. It never occurred to me to ask the Lord to help me with my weight problem, but when I did and He helped me to confess that I was an unmanageable glutton whose world revolved around food, I was wonderfully released of my uptight anger at the world. What a relief!

Anonymous

"I praise God for reaching into my entire life and showing me how He wants me to yield every part of it to Him. I did not realize how secretly rebellious my eating was nor how truly sinful I was until His light began to shine more clearly into my life. I was really fooling myself by blaming my problem on a weird metabolism. But the problem was me! I was without discipline.

"The best part was when I realized that God showed me all this hard truth in order to set me free to live by His power and in His will. Praise God, my eyes are being opened and my life is being changed!"

Julie Pascoe

For further information regarding the PACE-Weigh Ministry, including available materials, weight-control seminars, weekly classes, or speaking engagements, please write to Joan L. Cavanaugh, P.O. Box 487, Vista, California 92083.